Advance Praise for

A Man Left Albuquerque Heading East

"Susan Gerofsky's three-pronged inquiry into word problems offers a sophisticated and powerful analysis of these enduring cultural artifacts of mathematics teaching and learning. Readers will gain both in terms of the what and the why of these compact pedagogic devices and in terms of how to implement a linguistic-pragmatic perspective on mathematics education research—one which is gaining significantly in explanatory potential. Gerofsky's book deserves to be very widely read and re-read."

David Pimm, Professor, Department of Secondary Education,
Faculty of Education, University of Alberta, Canada

"Susan Gerofsky's delightful and insightful book should be read by all teachers of mathematics, and would also be of interest to almost anyone interested in engaging students in learning. She has taken as her subject the unlikely topic of word problems in mathematics and has unearthed a fascinating range of pedagogical richness. As a non-math person, I found the book fascinating, always instructive and entertaining. She treats the word problems as a kind of literary genre, and examines their history—going back at least 4,000 years—and their varied current uses. …In Gerofsky's concluding sections, she gives a number of practical suggestions for improving the use of word problems and the means to reconceive the genre. This is a profound, clear, and enjoyable book. It isn't often that one can recommend a study of math teaching as continually entertaining as well as practically valuable."

Kieran Egan, Canada Research Chair in Education,
Faculty of Education, Simon Fraser University

"In this insightful and cross-disciplinary examination of word problems, Susan Gerofsky makes an important and timely contribution to discussions of school mathematics through a provocative critique of such notions as meaningfulness and context. She soundly demonstrates that much of the rhetoric and many of the practices that surround such terms represent reformulation, not reform, of traditional emphases."

Brent Davis, Canada Research Chair in Mathematics Education and
the Ecology of Learning, Department of Secondary Education,
University of Alberta, Canada

A Man Left
Albuquerque
Heading East

extreme teaching
rigorous texts for troubled times

Joe L. Kincheloe and Danny Weil
General Editors

Vol. 5

PETER LANG
New York • Washington, D.C./Baltimore • Bern
Frankfurt am Main • Berlin • Brussels • Vienna • Oxford

Susan Gerofsky

A Man Left Albuquerque Heading East

Word Problems as Genre in Mathematics Education

PETER LANG
New York • Washington, D.C./Baltimore • Bern
Frankfurt am Main • Berlin • Brussels • Vienna • Oxford

Library of Congress Cataloging-in-Publication Data

Gerofsky, Susan.
A man left Albuquerque heading east: word problems as genre
in mathematics education / Susan Gerofsky.
p. cm. — (Extreme teaching: rigorous texts for troubled times. v. 5)
Includes bibliographical references and index.
1. Word problems (Mathematics). 2. Mathematics—Study and teaching.
I. Title. II. Series.
QA11.2 G47   510'.71—dc21   2002069269
ISBN 0-8204-5823-6
ISSN 1534-2808

Die Deutsche Bibliothek-CIP-Einheitsaufnahme

Gerofsky, Susan:
A man left Albuquerque heading east: word problems as genre
in mathematics education / Susan Gerofsky.
–New York; Washington, D.C./Baltimore; Bern;
Frankfurt am Main; Berlin; Brussels; Vienna; Oxford: Lang.
(Extreme teaching; Vol. 5)
ISBN 0-8204-5823-6

Cover design by Lisa Barfield
Cover photo by Phil Byrne

The paper in this book meets the guidelines for permanence and durability
of the Committee on Production Guidelines for Book Longevity
of the Council of Library Resources.

© 2004 Peter Lang Publishing, Inc., New York
275 Seventh Avenue, 28th Floor, New York, NY 10001
www.peterlangusa.com

Printed in the United States of America

To Phil, Adriana and Nicholas
and all our family
with love.

Table of Contents

Acknowledgments

Thanks to colleagues at Simon Fraser University and to members of the Canadian Mathematics Education Study Group for their support, challenges and stimulation.

A special and heartfelt "thank-you" to David Pimm for his thoughtful mentorship, excellent editorial advice and ongoing conversation about mathematics education. It is very much appreciated.

Many thanks to my terrific series editors, Shirley Steinberg and Joe Kincheloe, and to the editorial staff at Peter Lang.

Thanks to the teachers, students and curriculum writers who were interviewed for this book.

Work on this project was supported by a Canadian Social Sciences and Humanities Research Council (SSHRC) doctoral grant. The author would like to express gratitude to SSHRC and to Simon Fraser University for financial support.

The material in Chapter 3 first appeared in an article published in the journal *for the learning of mathematics*, and is reprinted by permission of the publisher:

Gerofsky, Susan. A linguistic and narrative view of word problems in mathematics education. *For the learning of mathematics, 16 (2)*, June 1996, 36–45. All rights reserved.

Chapter 1
Introduction

Overheard in a Finnish pancake restaurant in Thunder Bay, Ontario:

Child: OK, Mom, here's one for you. "A man left Albuquerque heading east at 55 miles per hour. At the same time, another man left Nashville heading west at 60 miles per hour. After some time the two men met. When they met, which man was closer to Nashville?"

Parent: Oh God, I hate these problems. OK, I think I can do it. Just let me get a pen. Pass that napkin. OK, here's Albuquerque and here's Nashville. Now the one guy is doing 55 going this way, and the other guy is doing 60 *that* way. We have to assume that there is a straight road between, what was it, Albuquerque and Memphis? Which I actually doubt. Why are these things always about American cities anyway?

Child: It's Nashville, but it doesn't matter. Anyway it sounds good. *Albuquerque.*

Parent: Bugs Bunny was always making a wrong turn at Albuquerque, wasn't he? Anyway, I guess the next step—you'd have to know how far it was between Albuquerque and Nashville.

Child: It doesn't matter.

Parent: It doesn't matter. Well, they don't give it to you, so you must be able to do it without it. So we'll just call it x. So it's x miles from one place to the other, and the one guy, we'll call him A, starts in Albuquerque and goes 55 miles an hour and the other guy, B, goes 60, so he would go farther, and so I guess guy A would be closer to Nashville. Right? God, I always hated these problems in school.

Child: Ha, ha, I got you! It doesn't matter how fast they went, because when they *met*, they would both be the same distance from Nashville! Get it?

Parent: [doubtful] Oh yeah ...

Child: Because they *met*, you see? So where they met, they were both in
the same spot. So they were the same distance from Nashville.

Parent: I still don't get it.

Mathematical word problems, or "story-problems," have long
been a familiar feature of school mathematics. For many students,
the transformation of word problems into arithmetic or algebra
causes great difficulty, and a number of recent studies have
addressed the linguistic and mathematical sources of that
difficulty from a psychological point of view (Burton, 1991; Harel
& Hoz, 1990 ; Hoz & Harel, 1990; Mangan, 1989; Ormell, 1991;
Plane, 1990; Puchalska & Semadeni, 1987).

There have also been a great many studies dating from the
mid-seventies onward that have looked at mathematical word
problems in terms of their "readability" (that is, the linguistic factors that make them easier or harder to read and understand) or
students' ease or difficulty in translating them from "normal language" to mathematical symbolism. (See, for example, Burton,
1991 and Nesher & Katriel, 1977.) Although such studies use linguistics to analyze word problems, they presuppose the value of
word problems as they are presently used in mathematics teaching and testing and the need for students to become more proficient at solving them.

Recent curriculum policy documents such as, for example, the
Cockcroft Report in Britain (DES, 1982, par. 243, quoted in
Prestage & Perks, 1992) and the NCTM Standards documents in
the United States (NCTM, 1989, 134–136) and many other national and provincial math curriculum documents (for example,
Alberta Education, 1999; Ontario Ministry of Education &
Training, 1999) call for curricular relevance and an emphasis on
the generic skills of problem solving. Many mathematics educators
have interpreted these imperatives as merely a call for more, better and more varied word problems. A few researchers (Borasi,

1986; Brown & Walter, 1990; Pinder, 1987) have begun to question the prevalent view that "problem solving" means exclusively the solution of word problems, and studies in ethnomathematics (Lave, 1988, 1992; Nunes, Schliemann & Carraher, 1993) have revealed that people who are successful and efficient mathematical problem-solvers in "real-life" (i. e., life outside of school) may be unable to solve school word problems with pencil and paper, even when these word problems appear to be similar to "real-life" problems that the person is quite capable of solving.

Paraphrase of an exchange overheard in an elementary school classroom (taken from Keitel, 1989, p. 7):

Teacher: Alright, class, here is a ratio problem for you. In order to paint a certain wall pink, a painter uses a gallon of white paint mixed with three drops of red paint. How much white and red paint would he use to paint a wall three times that size?

Student: Teacher, I know! My parents run a painting company, so I learned this from them. If you paint a really big wall, you have to mix the color a little bit darker, because the sunlight falling on a large wall will make the color appear lighter. And you would have to mix up the first gallon, and then mix the other batches to a chip, because there might be a slight color difference in different job lots of paint from the factory. In any case, you wouldn't mix up three batches of paint all at once, because the colors would start to separate before you were ready to use them. You're usually better to trust your eye than just to go by the measurements anyway…

Teacher: Alright! Enough! What you have to realize is that we're not talking about painting here, we're talking about ratio!

Yet word problems are firmly entrenched as a classroom tradition, particularly in North American schools. They figure prominently in virtually all school mathematics textbooks and in the previous school experience of those who are now teachers and curriculum developers and continue to be used unquestioningly by most teachers of school mathematics.

In this study of word problems in mathematics education, I consider mathematical word problems as a *genre*, using analytic theory from linguistics, literary criticism and mathematics education. I consider the question "what *are* word problems?" and try to answer it by "taking a walk" around the word-problem genre as an object in order to see it from many points of view, including the linguistic, the historical and the pedagogical.

This study is *not* intended to find ways to teach students to be more efficient solvers of mathematical word problems. Neither is it intended to use linguistic analysis to recommend better or more efficient ways to write word problems aimed at students of particular school grade levels or reading levels. Rather than ask "How can we make better word problems?" or "How can we make our students better solvers of word problems?," I ask, "What *are* word problems?"

My answers to this question follow from my observation that mathematical word problems can be seen as a linguistic and literary *genre* that forms part of the traditional pedagogy of mathematics. In Chapter 2 of this book, I write about the concept of genre itself, its cross-disciplinary origins and uses, and justify using the concept of genre in a study of word problems in mathematics education.

Considering a set of disparate texts as a genre is to view this set as a conceptual *object* (as in the term "mathematical object"). In metaphorical terms, my aim in this project is to see "the mathematical word problem" as a figure set against a variety of different backgrounds.

Since mathematical word problems are texts written in natural languages (although some would question how "natural" their language really is), I begin my walk around the word problem from the point of view of linguistics, in particular, the branch of linguistics called pragmatics, the study of language in use. From this point of view, word problems can be seen as a form of linguistic utterance, set against the background of all other forms of linguistic utterance. Certain oddities or particularities about the language of word problems can been seen from this point of view, including unusual forms of reference, an anomalous use of verb tense, and a particular discourse structure.

Problems of reference and truth value are evident in word problems generally. Examples like the following, where the words are clearly not meant to refer to the things they appear to point to, give clear instances of what is generally true of the word-problem genre:

> You walked for 20 km at 5 km/h. Later you returned running at 10 km/h. What was your average speed? (Kelly, Alexander & Atkinson, 1987b:, p. 136)

Here the second person pronoun is used to address and de-scribe, presumably, the reader. In this word problem, however, declarative statements about "you," the reader, clearly do not refer to me or probably to any actual readers of the problem. The problem could be restated in any of the following ways without changing its mathematical or pedagogical status as a word problem:

(a) (Stated hypothetically): Imagine that you walked for 20 km at 5 km/h, and that later you returned running at 10 km/h. What would your average speed have been?

(b) (Stated in the first person, presumably about the au-thor of the problem): I walked for 20 km at 5 km/h. Later I returned running at 10 km/h. What was my average speed?

(c) (Stated in the third person, about a fictional character or object):

Leslie walked for 20 km at 5 km/h. Later she returned running at 10 km/h. What was her average speed?

or: A horse walked for 20 km at 5 km/h. Later it returned running at 10 km/h. What was its average speed?

or: A train travels slowly down a track for 20 km at 5

km/h. Then it travels a further 20 km at 10 km/h. What is its average speed?

The equivalence of these various versions of the problem points out the indifference towards referentiality inherent in its story. For the writer or the teacher, it does not matter whether the reader or a horse or train, for that matter, would actually travel at 10 km/h nor whether the travel in question is a return trip or not. What matters is the mathematical structure seen to be underlying the various versions of the hypothetical story.

Nonetheless, the use of "you" in the original version of the question has a somewhat aggressive, accusatory tone. Other readers may respond to the statement "You walked ..." as I did, with an internal protestation of "No, I didn't!"

Word problems are also *story problems* and pose mathematical questions in the form of stories. So mathematical word problems can also be seen from the point of view of literature and narrative theory and can be viewed against a background of stories in general. Again certain peculiarities become evident, this time in terms of plot and character, the positioning of the narrator and reader, the placement of the narration in time and place—and these peculiarities are closely linked to word problems' linguistic features. In Chapter 3 I analyze mathematical word problems from the related points of view of linguistics and literary/narrative theory and find cohesion in the singular "object" seen from these two vantage points. The word-problem genre does indeed seem to be a unified, distinctive object, and this analysis provides suggestions as to which other genres it may be related to in terms of its linguistic and literary features.

Some word problems in my calculus textbook were difficult to approach, not because of the unfamiliarity of their subject matter but because their extreme whimsicality distracted me from approaching a solution method. For example:

33. A 160-lb man carries a 25-lb can of paint up a helical staircase that

encircles a silo with a radius of 20 ft. If the silo is 90 ft high and the man makes exactly three complete revolutions, how much work is done by the man against gravity climbing to the top?

34. Suppose there is a hole in the can of paint in Exercise 33 and 9 lb of paint leak steadily out of the can during the ascent. How much work is done? (Stewart, 1991, p. 866)

I found myself distracted by these stories to the point of being unable to consider the mathematics involved. I imagined nine pounds of paint—surely a large quantity of paint, perhaps a whole gallon!—dripping steadily down the helical staircase around the tall silo. Would the paint drip onto the silo itself, producing a kind of spiral action painting that visitors to the farm would admire, or would it drip steadily through the rungs of the stairway onto the cows below? When the man reached the top of the nine-storey silo and finally realized that more than a third of his paint was gone, would he curse and throw the rest of the bucket down after it? Or would he run back down the stairs with the leaky can, slip on the spilled paint and tumble the rest of the way down?

A description of genre requires us to ask not only, "What *is* it?" but also, "What is it *for*?" and "*Who* is it for?" Considerations of genre, at least since Bakhtin (1986), inevitably lead to questions of addressivity and intention. Addressivity refers to the author's real or imagined audience for a particular utterance or piece of writing. Bakhtin writes:

Both the composition and, particularly, the style of the utterance depend on those to whom the utterance is addressed, and the force of their effect on the utterance. Each speech [or written] genre in each area of … communication has its own typical conception of the addressee, and this defines it as a genre. (1986, p. 95)

In the case of word problems, intention includes educators' conscious, stated intentions when writing or teaching word problems but also intentions carried by the word-problem genre itself and students' uptake of their teachers' intentions, of which educators may not be aware. In Chapters 4, 5 and 6, I outline a small-scale empirical study in which I interviewed some teachers, students and curriculum writers in primary, secondary and tertiary mathematics education in order to begin to understand their intentions or uptake of others' intentions around the word-problem genre in mathematics education.

I saw this part of the study as a way of testing my analytic findings about word problems in conversation with others—students, teachers, writers—people who are intimately involved in the use of word problems in mathematics education. Again, there are many resonances with linguistics, since the study of linguistic pragmatics is deeply involved in questions of intentionality in language in use. As part of a walk around the word-problem genre, I take a standpoint in the practical, day-to-day world of mathematics pedagogy in schools and view the word-problem genre against a background of other pedagogic forms and intentions.

From an interview with a teacher of college calculus:

Teacher: I guess as I go through life I look for real-world situations that match the calculus I'm teaching. So when I saw some people playing with a model rocket in the park near my house, I thought, gee, that's like a linear motion problem in calculus. I was very familiar with problems from textbooks that addressed exactly the same abstract mathematical issues. And so it was easy enough to write it as a word problem.

Interviewer: Do you find you start seeing the world through "calculus eyes"? Do you focus your attention on things that are possible examples of the things that you're teaching?

Teacher: Yes. Very much so-... And yes, I do have the theoretical library stored there and then look for examples as they manifest themselves. And that's probably the factor that I use most in creating word problems.

Interviewer: What do you hope your students will take away with them once they've solved that particular problem or a whole bunch of problems? Do you want them to start looking at the world with calculus eyes too?

Teacher: Certainly. Yes. I would like them to be able to see mathematics in or project mathematics onto situations around them. What I try to do is say, well look, that abstract thing, we can see it here too, in the back-yard.

A final viewpoint in this study is a historical one. My questions here are, "What are the origins of the genre?" and "How has it changed over the course of its history?" Mathematical word problems have very ancient origins and a very long continuous history of use in the teaching and learning of mathematics. In Chapter 7, following on the analysis of earlier chapters, I look at the history of forms and intentions related to the word-problem genre. There is difficulty in ascribing particular intentions to written texts which span a very long history and wide-ranging cultural geography and which we are often obliged to read in translation. Nonetheless, there are at least some likely conjectures and intriguing suggestions to be gained from this point of view, looking at the word-problem genre as an object set against other historical texts in mathematics education.

From ancient Babylonian clay tablets, 4000 years old:

I found a stone, but did not weigh it; after I subtracted one-sixth and added one-third of one-eighth, I weighed it: 1 ma-na. What was the original weight of the stone? (Fauvel & Gray, 1987, p. 26)

How could someone subtract one-sixth of the weight of a stone if they hadn't weighed it in the first place? *Why* wouldn't they weigh it in the first place?

From the 3,500-year-old Rhind Mathematical Papyrus:

Houses, 7. Cats, 49 (7 X 7). Mice, 343 (7 X 7 X 7). Sheaves of wheat, 2401 (7 to the power 4). Hekats of grain, 16,807 (7 to the power 5). Total, 19,607. (Gillings, 1972, p. 169).

And an old English nursery rhyme:

As I was going to St. Ives, I met a man with seven wives.
Each wife had seven sacks, each sack had seven cats.
Each cat had seven kits.
Kits, cats, sacks, wives, how many going to St. Ives?

From the *Chiu-chang suan-shu*, from 3rd century B.C. China:

Two men starting from the same point begin walking in different directions. Their rates of travel are in the ratio 7:3. The slower man walks
toward the east. His faster companion walks to the south 10 pu and then
turns toward the northeast and proceeds until both men meet. How many
pu did each man walk? (Swetz & Kao, 1977, p. 45)

From an Italian Renaissance mathematics textbook:

The Holy Father sent a courier from Rome to Venice, commanding him
that he should reach Venice in 7 days. And the most illustrious Signoria
of Venice also sent another courier to Rome, who should reach Rome in 9
days. And from Rome to Venice is 250 miles. It happened that by order of
these lords the couriers started their journeys at the same time. It is required to find in how many days they will meet, and how many miles
each will have traveled. (Swetz, 1987, p. 158)

The so-called "two trains problem" existed two thousand years before
the invention of trains.

Finally, in Chapter 8, I suggest that an exploration of genre in
mathematics teaching and learning can be a source for innovation
and renewal in mathematics education practices. I propose that
identifying and describing the *genres*, or forms, of teaching can be
a creative step toward improving teaching. Knowing more about
educational genres allows us to take a more playful or artful attitude towards the forms that we have inherited. This aspect of
playing with forms is in contrast to the overwhelmingly moralizing
tone which has traditionally been central to educational writing. A
primarily moral stance tends to foreclose on the possibilities of a
genre with a stern "yea" or "nay" ("Use nothing but word-prob-

lems!" or "Never again use word-problems!") without ever taking the time to investigate what the genre is and why it is that way.

Knowing more about what a genre *is* in descriptive terms can allow us to play with the boundaries of the genre, changing or emphasizing its typical features and pushing it to the edge of its genre boundaries to create new forms. Knowing what a genre *is like* (i. e., what other genres it reminds us of or is structurally similar to) allows us to treat one genre *as if* it were another, to recontextualize it, and by placing an old genre in new settings, to give it new meanings by using analogy to other, similar genres.

Riddles, parables or word problems?

A poor man said to a rich one: "All my money goes on food."
"Now that's your trouble," said the rich man. "I only spend five per cent of my money on food."
—Sufi tale, from Shah, 1981, p. 51

The fiddler and his wife
The piper and his mother
Ate three cakes, three half cakes and three-quarters of another.
—Traditional British rhyme, from Opie & Opie, 1963, p. 72

A certain gentleman ordered that ninety measures of grain were to be moved from one of his houses to another, thirty half-leagues away. One camel was to transport the grain in three journeys, carrying thirty measures on each journey. A camel eats one measure each half-league. How many measures will be left, when all has been transported?
—from Alcuin of York, quoted in Olivastro, 1993, p. 131

Three sailors and their pet monkey are shipwrecked on an island. They spend all day gathering a pile of coconuts and decide to divide them in the morning. But in the night, one sailor awakes and decides to take his third. He divides the pile into three equal parts, but there is one coconut extra, which he gives to the monkey. He then takes and hides his third and puts the rest back in a pile. Then another wakes up and does exactly the same, and then the third. In the morning, they divide the pile that remains into three equal parts, again finding one extra coconut, which they give to the monkey. How many coconuts were there at the start?

—Ganita-sara-sangrata, Mahavira, India, 850 A.D., Olivastro, 1993, p. 180

Knowing some of the *intentions* encoded within a generic form, knowing *whom* it is addressing and some of what it is striving to say to its intended audience, allows us to know what a particular genre will or will not allow us to say by its very form. An awareness of codified intentions allows us to play with various ways of saying what (we think) we intend.

Finally, understanding something of the history of a genre, knowing where a genre *comes from*, allows us to retrieve cultural memories, to revive old meanings in new settings and make new meanings in old settings. Revisiting archaic forms and intentions can give inspiration and energy in the present.

Chapter 2
What Is Meant by Genre?

In this study I consider mathematical word problems as an object, set as a figure in the ground of other textual, literary and linguistic forms. That is to say, I look at "the mathematical word problem" as a literary and linguistic *genre*. Since the concept of *genre* is seldom invoked in discussions of mathematics education, I want to discuss its implications further here.

Many writers (for example, Buscombe, 1970/1995; Palmer, 1991; Sobchack, 1975/1995) credit Aristotle with outlining the first notions of genre in Western culture. In the *Poetics*, Aristotle tried to establish a comprehensive set of categories that would encompass all types of poetry (tragic, epic, lyric, etc.), along with definitions and rules for each of these categories, an analysis of the function of each poetic type and a ranking of their relative importance. Aristotle's universalist, taxonomic program dominated studies of literary types until at least the eighteenth century, and its influence is still felt in modern attempts to create comprehensive lists of "types" of oral and written literature (for example, folklorists' motif-index or tale-type index, cited in Scott, 1965, p. 17).

Bakhtin and Genre

Most contemporary uses of genre, however, have developed in relation to M. M. Bakhtin's notion of *speech genres*. The work of Bakhtin (1894–1975), the Russian literary critic and philosopher of language, has been tremendously influential in contemporary Anglo–American literary and linguistic studies even though much of his work has only recently been translated into English. Bakhtin's essay on "The Problem of Speech Genres" (Bakhtin, 1986, pp. 60–102), written in 1952–53, became available in English in the mid-1970s and has influenced theoretical developments in the fields of film studies, folklore studies and linguistics as well as literary criticism.

Bakhtin's concept of genre takes in a very wide range of language phenomena, oral and written, from both "high" and "low" culture. Bakhtin stresses "the extreme *heterogeneity* of speech genres, oral and written" and cites as examples of speech genres everything from "short rejoinders of everyday dialogue" and "everyday narration" to "business documents, ... the diverse forms of scientific statements and all literary genres (from the proverb to the multivolume novel)." (pp. 60–61)

Bakhtin's basic unit of analysis is the *utterance*, a unit of language in use and in context, which Bakhtin differentiates from structural linguistics' *ideal sentence*, which is postulated as a decontextualized entity. Any utterance, from a verbal greeting to an epic poem, is addressed to another person or persons, even if this audience or partner is imagined by the speaker or writer. Bakhtin stresses the dialogic nature of all oral and written language—even monologue is framed as a form of dialogue—and sees the quality of *addressivity*, of addressing a known or imagined other, as key to the understanding of utterances. The boundaries of the Bakhtinian utterance are defined in terms of addressivity. The end of an utterance is signalled by a change of speakers or by the end of a particular piece of written discourse at the point where "the speaker has said (or written) everything he wishes to say at a particular moment or under particular circumstances" and there exists for the addressee "the possibility of responding to it" (p. 76). So an utterance may be extremely short (for example, a sentence fragment or exclamation uttered as part of the turn-taking activity of a verbal conversation) or very long (as in the "utterance," in writing, of a long novel or a Ph.D. thesis). Bakhtin sees the listener or audience not as a passive partner in dialogue but as a force constantly shaping the utterance of the speaking or writing subject through the listener/reader's forthcoming or anticipated response. So, in Bakhtin's theory, speech and writing can never be removed from a context of addressivity, of dialogue. There is always a ground for the (linguistic) figure although the same figure can be reframed in terms of different grounds.

For Bakhtin, there is no possibility of utterances that exist outside of genre—"that is," he writes, "all our utterances have definite and relatively stable typical *forms of construction of the whole*" (p. 78). Like Molière's Monsieur Jourdain, who had no idea he was speaking in prose, Bakhtin writes, we "speak in diverse genres without suspecting that they exist" (p. 78). Bakhtin stresses that although genres are relatively stable forms comprising appropriate contexts, styles, formats and other features, it would be futile to attempt a comprehensive taxonomy of genres within a language and culture because new genres are always developing (and, presumably, some genres are becoming obsolete or less used). Bakhtin writes:

> The wealth and diversity of speech genres are boundless because the various possibilities of human activity are inexhaustible, and because each sphere of activity contains an entire repertoire of speech genres that differentiate and grow as the particular sphere develops and becomes more complex. (p. 60)

So Bakhtin's conception of genre can be characterized by: a heterogeneous grouping of "high" and "low," oral and written, short and long language forms; an emphasis on the constitutive nature of addressivity and the dialogic nature of language; an insistence on the unavoidability of context; definition of the utterance as the basic unit of analysis; the assertion that no utterance can exist outside the generic forms of a language; and a recognition of genre as a productive class within language, an ever-changing inventory of relatively stable forms.

Genre Ideas from Film Studies

The field of film studies, which was growing and gaining academic legitimacy in the 1970s, took up the Bakhtinian concept of genre as a necessary construct for dealing theoretically with a relatively stable repertoire of film types (Neale, 2000, p. 10). Genre was originally used in a slightly derogatory sense to categorize the popular formula films (often so-called "B movies") produced by the Hollywood film industry (for example, Westerns, gangster films, musicals or screwball comedies). However, the term was soon extended to include genres like art films, the French New Wave, docudramas and other less commercial but generically recognizable types of films. In film studies, the notion of the utterance was greatly extended to include other non-linguistic visual and sound resources (camerawork, direction, acting, editing, sound effects, music, etc.) as well as a complex of cultural forms connected with the addressivity of films (including distribution and exhibition patterns, film advertising and promotion, and so on).

Film genre theorists have raised issues that will be useful in my discussion of the mathematical word-problem as genre. For example, Tudor, in his well-known essay on genre (Tudor, 1973/1995) puts forth the problem of the "empiricist dilemma" in identifying genres—in this case, the "Western" genre in popular films. "To take a genre such as a Western, analyze it, and list its principal characteristics is to beg the question that we must first isolate the body of films that are Westerns," writes Tudor. But such films can only be isolated according to their principal characteristics.

> We are caught in a circle that first requires that the films be isolated, for which purposes a criterion is necessary, but the criterion is, in turn, meant to emerge from the empirically established common characteristics of the films. (Tudor, p. 5).

Tudor's suggestion for a way out of this dilemma is to avoid establishing *a priori* criteria and instead to "lean on a common cultural consensus as to what constitutes a Western and then go on to analyze it in detail" (p. 5). This solution presupposes a high degree of shared culture and the likelihood of shared patterns of recognition and meanings that are part of that culture. Tudor suggests that "from a very early age most of us have built up a picture of a Western. We feel that we know a Western when we see one …" (p. 5) So to call a film a Western is more than to define it as sharing certain principal characteristics with other Westerns; it also suggests that the film would be more or less universally recognized as a Western in our culture. Tudor writes, "Genre notions … are not critics' classifications made for special purposes; they are sets of cultural conventions. Genre is what we collectively believe it to be" (p. 7).

I invoke this notion of culturally recognizable convention and form in my analysis of mathematical word-problems as genre. I contend that the form and addressivity of word problems, at least as they are used in twentieth-century mathematics education, is recognizable nearly universally among, say, Canadians who have been students in public elementary schools, and I daresay they are also recognizable in a similar way to most people of all cultures who have attended formal school mathematics classes. The extraordinarily long history of word problems (they appear to have been used continuously for four thousand years, at least since ancient Babylonian and Egyptian times) seems to suggest that they have existed as a cultural form since the development of the earliest writing systems although it is important not to read our meanings anachronistically on earlier cultures. As Tudor cautions,

> There is no basis for assuming that a Western [or in our case, the word-problem genre] will be conceived in the same way in every culture. The way in which the genre term is applied can quite conceivably vary from case to case (p. 7).

Film critic Steve Neale (Neale, 2000) quotes literary critic E. D. Hirsch in another characterization of genre that applies equally to literature, linguistics, film theory and the genres of schooling. Neale writes that Hirsch

> insists on the fact that genres centrally include—even consist of—a set of expectations. A reader's or interlocutor's "preliminary generic

conception", he writes, "is constitutive of everything that he subsequently understands ...". (Neale, 2000, p. 23).

Neale writes further that

> Genres do not consist solely of films. They consist also of specific systems of expectation and hypothesis which spectators bring with them to the cinema and which interact with films themselves during the course of the viewing process. These systems provide spectators with means of recognition and understanding. They help render individual films, and the elements within them, intelligible and, therefore, explicable. They offer a way of working out the significance of what is happening on the screen: a way of working out why particular actions are taking place. (p. 31)

Similarly, "curriculum genres" in schooling (viz. Berkenkotter & Huckin, 1995, pp. 151–163), do not consist solely of the texts or utterances observable in classrooms. A curricular genre like mathematical word problems consists as well of the "specific systems of expectation and hypothesis" which students learn early in their school careers and subsequently bring with them to mathematics classes. Teachers and curriculum writers bring similar expectations to the processes of writing and teaching and this meeting place of text, intention and expectation actually constitutes the genre. It allows students and teachers to make sense of word problems, despite their inherent oddness both as stories and as mathematical exercises. It allows students to work out what is probable, plausible and likely to occur in a particular word problem and also what is likely to be expected of them in their response to the problem. It makes possible actions on the part of students which will be deemed intelligent, appropriate, laudable and not foolish or excessive. Familiarity with genre expectations allows students to "save face" and to function smoothly and successfully within the culture of the school, where some very strange artefacts like word problems are presented to them.

In chapter 3, I will discuss in detail the expectations that readers (and writers) of word problems bring to that genre in terms of the intentions coded within word problems and interpreted within their context of use. These intentions, at least as they are "read" in some contemporary classrooms, are further interrogated in Chapters 5 and 6. Intentionality in linguistic genres is discussed in terms of the "force" of an utterance or text—that is to say, its literal meaning, its intended effect on the listener/ reader, the reader or listener's interpretation of that intention and what ends the utterance actually accomplishes as a "speech act." Expectations and intentions with regard to mathematical word problems, as with film and literary genres, turn out to be central factors in the consideration of their meanings, their use and their role in culture, in this case, the culture of the classroom.

Another film critic, Sobchack (1975/1995) considers well-established "B-movie" film genres in terms of their relationship to the classical literary forms outlined by Aristotle. He writes that such well-established genre films as Westerns, detective movies and musicals operate on the same principle as Greek dramas in that they are reshapings of already-known tales. If Greek dramas are "imitations of fictions," then genre films

> … are made in imitation not of life but of other films. True, there must be the first instance in a series or cycle, yet most cases of the first examples of various film genres can be traced to literary sources, primarily pulp literature. … And once the initial film is made, it has entered the pool of common knowledge known by filmmaker and film audience alike. Imitations and descendants—the long line of "sons of," "brides of," and "the return of"—begin. (p. 104)

There is an interesting parallel here with the question of word problem as genre. If word problems follow the pattern established by literary and film genres, then are they written "in imitation, not of life, but of other word problems"? I firmly believe this to be the case and I think this is a sad but necessary realization for those mathematics educators who try, sincerely, to write word problems that more closely imitate life or relate to the lived experiences of their students. I contend that the genre form itself speaks directly to the students in terms of what is given them and expected of them; readers dive into the world created by the genre as into a familiar (warm or ice-cold) bath. Word problems imitate and re-call other word problems, not our lived lives.

Ultimately, Sobchack raises questions of addressivity in terms of audience expectations. He writes about genre films and their "insistence on the familiar. It is what we expect in a genre film and what we get" (p. 105). He emphasizes the cathartic satisfaction we get as an audience in seeing the old familiar stories of our culture replayed, with familiar and formulaic spots for tears, screams, white knuckles and laughter. Again there is a parallel with students' responses to word problems, although the familiarity of the response is as likely to be neurotic as cathartic. For those who like word problems and have figured out how to "be good at them," there is a great deal of pleasure in decoding their hidden mathematical message, performing the required operations and re-coding the answer till it matches the one at the back of the book. For those who hate word problems (and the genre does seem to evoke only extremes of emotion), the familiarity of the genre may evoke familiar feelings of panic, helplessness and self-doubt.

Finally, Sobchack emphasizes genre films' conservatism in matters of form and

> profound respect for Aristotelian dramatic values. There is always a definite sense of beginning, middle and end, of closure and of a frame. The film begins with "Once upon a time ..." and ends only after all the strings have been neatly tied, all major conflicts resolved. It is a closed world. There is little room in the genre film for ambiguity anywhere. (pp. 105–106)

A similar conservatism of form and sense of a "closed world" is evident in the word-problem genre. My question, which will be addressed in the last chapter of this book, is how to work against generic expectations while retaining aspects of a very conservative form—how to open up what has been a closed form by seeing it against a different ground, for example, the ground of story or of language.

Genre Ideas from Linguistics, Folklore Studies and Literary Theory

Bakhtin's concept of genre arose from his work in literary criticism and linguistics and theorists in these fields have also taken up Bakhtinian terms (though perhaps with less alacrity than film theorists, since linguists and critics may have seen Bakhtin's ideas as antagonistic to other, established analytic methods). Folklore studies, another newly-legitimized academic discipline, has also adopted elements of Bakhtinian analysis. All three fields have in common a need to account for chunks of language larger than the sentence and concepts of utterance and genre have lent themselves well to certain kinds of theory.

Rather than try to give a complete account of genre ideas used in linguistics, literature study or folklore, I will borrow from work in these fields and find concepts that are useful in analyzing mathematical word problems. In scavenging from a number of disciplines, I am looking for a larger interdisciplinary construct of genre, which I believe is consonant with Bakhtin's intentions in his original introduction of the term.

Earlier, I mentioned Tudor's insistence that genres should not be defined solely by means of an *a priori* list of characteristics but by cultural consensus and familiarity as well. Other theorists also argue from different perspectives against the strict analytic definition of genre.

Palmer (1991), a literary theorist, makes a distinction between two broad categories of analyses of historical genres:

> ... studies in which what is sought is a tight, exclusive definition where the boundaries between belonging and not belonging to a genre are clear; and studies where a loose definition is sought, where genre is not a precisely ordered group of texts, but an approximation, a horizon of expectations for the readership, a series of imprecise "echoes" between texts ... (pp. 121–122)

Palmer favors the second, looser characterization of genre, which allows for a degree of variation within what is still a culturally recognizable category—perhaps a category with fuzzy edges.

The linguist Swales (1990) also questions whether or not categories in language and linguistic forms can be tightly defined by a list of traits all must share. He quotes rhetoricians Campbell and Jamieson aiming to "illumine rather than classify" when they discuss the "constellation of features" that define generic forms:

> A genre is a group of acts unified by a constellation of forms that recurs in each of its members. These forms, *in isolation*, appear in other discourses. What is distinctive about the acts in a genre is a recurrence of the forms *together* in constellation. (Campbell & Jamieson, 1978, quoted in Swales, 1990, p. 43)

Swales also cites work in category theory (originally from anthropology but adopted by linguistic semantics), particularly the work of Rosch. Rosch (1975) argues for an internal structure for categories, so that not all members of a category have equal status (as opposed to the mathematical notion of a set, in which all members meet definitional criteria and thus have equal membership status). For example, ostriches, parrots, chickens, penguins, sparrows and robins are all birds but some seem "birdier" than others to most people within a culture. Rosch's studies showed that, for Americans, a robin seemed far closer to the central idea of "bird" than did a penguin, for example. Similarly, Americans saw apples and plums as more typical of the category "fruits" than olives and coconuts. Rosch calls the most culturally central examples of a category *prototypes* and the least central examples *marginal*. Marginal members of a category have a lower probability of being included in the category although they may share definitional characteristics assigned to the category (both robins and ostriches have feathers and wings and lay eggs). Swales writes:

> Organisms like bats and whales are problematic because they carry
> properties that meet high probability expectations of categories to which
> they do not technically belong. (p. 52)

I will explore the idea of central and marginal genre membership further in my analysis of the mathematical word-problem
genre. With Rosch and Palmer, I am cautious not to try to create
an exclusive, watertight definition for genre membership but instead to outline a "constellation of features" that co-occur in central exemplars of the genre. I am also interested in the directions
we can find as educators in exploring the marginal, borderline areas—those areas where membership in the category or genre is
fuzzy. By pushing generic borders and playing against type in
terms of a number of variables, we can extend our ways of seeing
and working with fixed generic forms, generate new forms and
practices in education and perhaps bring into focus the usually
invisible grounds of traditional mathematics education.

Swales quotes another rhetorical scholar, Miller (1984). Miller
writes:

> To consider as potential genres such homely discourse as the letter of
> recommendation, the user manual, the progress report ... [and I would
> add here "the word problem"] is not to trivialize the study of genres; it is
> to take seriously the rhetoric in which we are immersed and the situa-
> tions in which we find ourselves. (p. 155)

and argues that:

> ... what we learn when we learn a genre is not just a pattern of forms or
> even a method of achieving our own ends. We learn, more importantly,
> what ends we may have. (p. 165)

This speaks most cogently to the acculturating power of forms
within mathematics education and education generally—that
generic forms, which are familiar and recognizable but often existing below the threshold of our conscious recognition, define us in

our relationship to our worlds. Through genre forms, we learn what may be asked and what is beyond question in our culture, what we may aspire to and what is outlandish or forbidden. Questioning and exerting pressure on genre is a way of questioning particular unspoken boundaries of culture and this is especially important when working in a culture like that of school mathematics, with a strong tradition of conservatism and exclusion.

Chapter 3
What *Is* a Word Problem?

Jake and Jerry went on a camping trip with their motorcycles. One day Jerry left camp on his motorcycle to go to the village. Ten minutes later Jake decided to go too. If Jerry was travelling 30 mph and Jake traveled 35 mph, how long before Jake caught up with Jerry?

—Johnson, 1992, p. 28

A person bought oranges at the rate of 36 cents a dozen; had he received 6 more for the same money they would have cost him 6 cents a dozen less. How many did he buy?

—1902 Public School Leaving Examination of the Northwest Territories, in NCTM, 1970, p. 419

There is supposed a lawe made that (for furtheryng of tyllage) every man that doth kepe shepe, shall for every 10 shepe eare and sowe one acre of grounde, and for his allowance in sheepe pasture there is appointed for every 4 shepe one acre of pasture. Nowe is there a ryche shepemaister whyche hath 7000 akers of grounde, and would gladlye kepe as manye sheepe as he myght by that statute. I demaunde howe many shepe shall he kepe?

—Robert Record, *The Ground of Artes*, 1552, in Fauvel & Gray, 1987, p. 278

1,000 loaves of pesu 5 are to be exchanged, a half for loaves of pesu 10, and a half for loaves of pesu 20. How many of each will there be?

—Rhind Mathematical Papyrus, Problem 74, in Gillings, 1972, p. 130

Per b`ur [surface unit] I have harvested 4 gur of grain. From a second b`ur I have harvested 3 gur of grain. The yield of the first field was 8,20 more than that of the second. The area of the two fields were together 30,0. How large were the fields?

—Babylonian document VAT 8389, Berlin Museum; translation from van der Waerden, 1954 , p. 66

In this chapter, I will establish a description of the mathematical word problem as a linguistic genre, particularly considering its pragmatic structure. Through a description of the pragmatics and discourse features of the genre and through comparison of the word-problem genre to other spoken and literary genres, I hope to find clues to the unspoken assumptions underlying its use and nature as a medium of instruction.

In this chapter, I *problematize* the use of word problems in mathematics education. I look at word problems as a linguistic and literary genre and describe the features of that genre. By "making them strange," seeing word problems in a new way, my intention is to make the word-problem genre a conceptual object that we will be able to circle around, look at from different perspectives and compare usefully with other conceptual objects (for example, other literary and cultural genres).

Areas of Linguistics Used in This Study

Contemporary linguistics has gone through many changes as a discipline since its origins at the turn of the century and many significant changes have taken place over the past fifteen years. Useful areas recently accepted into mainstream linguistics, such as pragmatics (the study of language in use in particular contexts), discourse analysis (the study of extended stretches of spoken or written text in terms of utterances and their relationships), sociolinguistics (the study of language and social class and power relationships), semantics (the study of the fields of word meanings), dialectology (the study of varieties of language, their distribution and history), stylistics (the study of literary texts in terms of their linguistic features) and genre studies (the study of "text types" in terms of their linguistic and contextual features), have recently become available to mathematics education researchers. For example, Roth (1996) uses conversational analysis as a way of analyzing discourse, to look at the sociology of mathematics students' learning when dealing with "real-life" problems and word problems and Rowland (1992, 1999) and Pimm (1987, 1995) apply new developments in pragmatics, particularly questions of *deixis*, or "pointing with words," to mathematics education.

In this study, I use methods from pragmatics, discourse analysis and genre studies to try to shed light on the nature of word problems as applications of mathematics and as stories. (Readers looking for definitions and examples of specialized terminology may wish to consult the glossary of terms from linguistics, discourse and genre analysis in the Appendix.)

Word Problems and Their Three-Component Structure

> You receive a paycheck worth $125.50. You must give 1/5 of your earnings to both the provincial and federal government. How much money do you have left? (Word problem written by a grade 6 student in Vancouver, reported in Menon, 1993).

Most word problems, whether from ancient or modern sources, follow a three-component compositional structure:

1) A "set-up" component, establishing the characters and location of the putative story. (This component is often not essential to the solution of the problem.)
2) An "information" component, which gives the information needed to solve the problem (and sometimes extraneous information as a decoy for the unwary).
3) A question.

Variations on this structure occur; for example, the set-up and information components are sometimes collapsed into one sentence by the use of subordinate clauses, or the information component and the question are collapsed into a single sentence by using a subjunctive "if ... then" structure.

Johnson addresses this structure explicitly in her interesting little instructional book, *How to Solve Word Problems in Algebra* (Johnson, 1992). Her advice to students who are having trouble with the transformation of word problems into algebra includes the following:

> Look for a question at the end of the problem. This is often a good way to find what you are solving for ... What you are trying to find is usually stated in the question at the end of the problem ... Simple problems generally have two statements. One statement helps you set up the unknowns and the other gives you equation information. Translate the problem from words to symbols a piece at a time. (pp. 1–2)

Wickelgren (1974), in another book on mathematical problem solving, also identifies three parts to mathematical problems in general and these fit closely with the three-part structure proposed for word problems:

> All the formal problems of concern to us can be considered to be composed of three types of information: information concerning *givens* (given expressions), information concerning *operations* that transform one or more expressions into one or more new expressions and information concerning *goals* (goal expressions). (p. 10)

In terms of the three components typical of word problems, the first component generally contains none of Wickelgren's three types of information; the second component contains the *givens* and sometimes the *operations.* The operations, however, are often left unstated, since word problems are usually grouped together as a practice set for a particular set of algorithms that are currently the focus of classroom teaching. The choice of the correct algorithm from the currently active set is considered one of the student's main responsibilities; to give the operation explicitly in the problem would be considered giving away too much. The third component, the question, identifies the *goals* of the problem.

The three-component structure of typical word problems seems, then, to be based on the structure of arithmetic algorithms or algebraic problems rather than on the conventions of oral or written storytelling. In the case of an algebraic word problem, the student is required to write an algebraic equation in terms of a set of variables which are related to one another in a fixed (or "fixable") relationship that can be stated in terms of an equality or inequality. To "solve" the algebraic problem, the student must know which term to isolate (the *goal* or "the unknown"). This information is given (sometimes implicitly) in components two and three of algebraic word problems, which could be paraphrased as follows.

> **Component 2:** The variables or quantities *A, B, C,* ... are in the following relationship ... (and you must deduce from the context of your lessons and the problem itself what operations are necessary to set up the equation).
> **Component 3:** Solve for variable (*X*).

Component 1 of a typical word problem is, so far as I can see, simply an alibi, the only nod toward "story" in the story problem. It sets up a situation for a group of characters, places and objects that is generally irrelevant to the writing and solving of the arithmetic or algebraic problem embedded in later components. In fact, too much attention to story will distract students from the translation task at hand, leading them to consider "extraneous" factors from the story rather than concentrating on extracting variables and operations from the more mathematically salient components 2 and 3.

It is important to ask why the first component is included in word problems at all, or why this "translation" or "transformation" exercise should be considered important for one's mathematical studies. Many writers consider such problems to be practically useful, at least by analogy. Johnson (1992) writes:

> You will find certain basic types of word problems in almost every algebra book. You can't go out and use them in daily life, or in electronics, or in nursing. But they teach you *basic procedures* which you will be able to use elsewhere. (p. 1)

On the other hand, Kubala (1973), in *Practical Problems in Mathematics for Electricians*, makes direct claims for the usefulness of the problems he presents:

> The student learning electrical theory and wiring practices will find that
> by using Practical Problems In Mathematics For Electricians his under-
> standing of various mathematics principles will be reinforced because of
> their use in problems frequently encountered by an electrician .... Any
> student in a program of instruction in electricity will benefit from the use
> of this related problems workbook. Practicing electricians who desire to
> improve their math skills will also find it helpful. (p. 4)

It has been documented that the nature of the stories attached
to the algebraic problems is relevant to students in terms of affect
and in terms of the student's willingness to try to solve the problem at all (Sowder, 1989; Pimm, 1995). It is also interesting to note
that, over the course of several years, students become encultur-
ated in the world of school mathematics and familiar with the
conventions of the word-problem genre to the extent that they are
able to reproduce it. Menon (1993) documents word problems in
canonical form written by elementary school students who were
asked to formulate their own mathematical questions. Menon also
cites Ellerton's (1989) large-scale study of 10,000 secondary students in Australia and New Zealand who, when asked to write
one difficult word problem, overwhelmingly wrote problems similar in form to those in their textbooks. Lave (1992) has noted:

> If you ask children to make up problems about everyday math they will
> not make up problems about their experienced lives, they will invent ex-
> amples of the genre; they too know what a word problem is. (p. 77)

Puchalska & Semadeni (1987) comment that, while younger elementary school children often believe, naively, that the stories in
story problems are relevant, more experienced older children know
better.

Radatz (1984) points out that, during problem solving, school
beginners concentrate on stories rather than on numbers; during interviews it has been found that such children often augment the
story with what follows from their own knowledge or experience.
Older children, however, always try to reach some solution, per-

haps by a trial-and-error strategy and they often believe that nothing is unsolvable in mathematics. Children with little mathematical experience try to analyze the story more carefully, whereas older students have a specific attitude towards mathematics: It is viewed as an activity with artificial rules and without any specific relation to out-of-school reality. (p. 10)

Word Problems, Intentions and Speech Acts: Locutionary, Illocutionary and Perlocutionary Force and Uptake

Questions about the perceived purpose of the textbook writer or teacher in presenting word problems or the student in solving them relate to notions in pragmatics called **locutionary, illocutionary** and **perlocutionary force**, which are, in turn, part of speech act theory. J. L. Austin, the philosopher of language who originated speech act theory, saw the need for an analysis of language in the context of interactions, so that not only the literal meaning of an utterance but its meaning as action could be considered. Austin writes:

> We may be quite clear what "Shut the door" means, but not yet at all clear on the further point as to whether as uttered at a certain time it was an order, an entreaty or whatnot. What we need besides the old doctrine about meaning is a new doctrine about all the possible forces of utterances, towards the discovery of which our proposed list of explicit performative verbs would be a very great help. (Austin, quoted in Levinson, 1983, p. 236)

Austin identified three kinds of speech acts that are simultaneously performed in an utterance:

> 1) a **locutionary act**: the utterance of a sentence with determinate sense and reference
> (2) an **illocutionary act**: the making of a statement, offer, promise, etc. in uttering a sentence, by virtue of the conventional *force* associated with it (or with its explicit performative paraphrase)
> (3) a **perlocutionary act**: the bringing about of effects on the

audience by means of uttering the sentence, such effects being special
to the circumstances of the utterance (Levinson, 1983, p. 236)

Levinson gives the example of the sentence, "You can't do
that," which has a literal meaning (its locutionary force) and
which may have the illocutionary force of protesting to the person
being addressed but the perlocutionary force of either checking the
addressee's action, or bringing the addressee to his or her senses,
or simply annoying the person.

Levinson differentiates between the perlocutionary force of an
utterance, which is specific to the circumstances of issuance and
the consequences of an illocutionary act, which include the understanding of the illocutionary force by the addressee(s). In the case
of word problems, the perlocutionary force would include questions of affect in the individual learner (the intended or unintended effect of stimulating or boring, encouraging or discouraging,
attracting or frightening or disgusting or delighting a particular
learner, for example) and Levinson quotes Austin as admitting
that perlocutionary force is often indeterminate or indeterminable.
(Levinson, 1983, p. 237) However, the uptake or understanding of
the illocutionary force in word problems by learners deserves further consideration.

Questions about the perceived purpose of the textbook writer
in presenting word problems or the student in solving them relate
to locutionary, illocutionary and perlocutionary force (that is, the
literal meaning, the performative intention and the effect upon the
audience of an utterance). Applying this analysis to word problems poses some problems in terms of their locutionary force because of problems relating to deixis. As discussed later (in the
sections on verb tense and the Gricean maxim of quality), word
problems do not generally have referents—that is to say, they do
not refer to "real-life" objects, people or places in any but the
most arbitrary way. This could conceivably place word problems
in the category of fiction, but I would argue that they are so
deficient in the rudiments of plot, character, dramatic tension,

poetic use of language, moral or social theme, etc., as to be very poor fiction at best. (The metaphor "word problems as parable" will be discussed later.) For the moment, I would prefer to view mathematical problems as a genre unto themselves with *indeterminate* locutionary force.

Their illocutionary force seems to be quite directly accessible to students with sufficient enculturation in the genre; it is "Solve this!" or "Find X!" This command brings with it certain underlying assumptions:

- that "this" is solvable:
- that X can be found;
- that the word problem itself contains all the information needed to do this task;
- that no information extraneous to the problem may be sought (apart from conventional mathematical operations which likely must be supplied);
- that the task can be achieved using the mathematics that the student has access to;
- that the problem has been provided to get the student to practice an algorithm recently presented in their math course;
- that there is a single correct mathematical interpretation of the problem;
- that there is one right answer;
- that the teacher can judge an answer to be correct or incorrect;

and especially,

- that the problem can be reduced to mathematical form—in fact, that the problem is at heart an arithmetic or algebraic formulation which has been "dressed up" in words and that the student's job is to "undress" it again—to transform the words back into the arithmetic or algebra that the writer was thinking of, then to solve the problem.

Students' uptake or understanding of the illocutionary force in word problems is, I think, quite clear and could be paraphrased by a learner as follows:

> I am to ignore component 1 and any story elements of this problem, use the math we have just learned to transform components 2 and 3 into the correct arithmetic or algebraic form, solve the problem to find the one correct answer and then check that answer with the correct answer in the back of the book or turn it in for correction by the teacher, who knows the translation and the answer.

In this light, Puchalska & Semadeni's (1987) finding that children who were experienced in school math tried somehow to solve word problems which had missing, surplus or contradictory data is not at all surprising. I contend that these children had a well-developed schema with regard to word problems which included many facets of the genre, including its illocutionary force and that a command to "make sense of this story in terms of everyday life" or to "search for deficiencies or contradictions in this problem" was never conceived as part of that illocutionary force (for the students or indeed, for most teachers and textbook writers).

The Question of "Truth Value"

The term "truth value" was introduced into semantics by Frege and Strawson and was adopted from semantics into pragmatics. Frege wanted to be able to evaluate the meaning of all statements in terms of a principle of bivalence—that is, if something was not true, it was false and if not false, it must be true. (This principle is familiar to anyone working with mathematical proofs, where the "law of the excluded middle" allows for the possibility of proofs by contradiction.)

There are problems with Frege's notion of truth value, particularly when it is applied to utterances other than the propositional statements of philosophy. For example, questions, imperatives and exclamations cannot be assessed for truth value. The truth value (if any) of statements in the context of fiction (storytelling, novels, plays, etc.) is also problematic. Lamarque & Olsen (1994,

p. 54) give the following statements which might occur in a work of fiction:

(a) John worked in the fields;
(b) He found it tiring;
(c) There was once a young man who worked in the fields;
(d) Working in the fields is tiring.

They consider that, while statements (c) and (d) might be assessed for truth value if construed outside of the context of the work of fiction (unlike (a) and (b)), this ignores the proper contextual construal of these statements. They give "a common alternative to the falsity thesis" in dealing with statements in fiction, which is the "no-truth-value" view of fictive utterance, partly attributed to Frege and Strawson. Three versions of this view are:

1. Sentences in works of fiction are neither true nor false because their (existential) presuppositions are false;
2. Sentences in works of fiction are neither true nor false because the sentences are not asserted;
3. It is inappropriate (mistaken, etc.) to ascribe truth or falsity to sentences in works of fiction. (Lamarque & Olsen, 1994, p. 57)

Lamarque and Olsen resort to a description of fictive utterances as pretense, or writing "as if" something were true and distinguish three types of pretense: pretending to *be* ..., pretending to *do* ... and pretending *that* .... It is here that I can situate word problems; they pretend *that* a particular story situation exists. What is more, to paraphrase Lamarque and Olsen, readers of word problems must pretend *that* such a situation exists, *under instruction from the writer of the word problem*. Further, students "must pretend *that someone is telling them*" about that situation (Lamarque & Olsen, 1994, p. 71, authors' emphasis). The reader's response is not in terms of truth value but mimesis, yet at the same time the story is considered disposable, interchangeable with other equivalent stories which would certainly not be the case with a work of fiction.

Linguistic and Metalinguistic Verb Tense

Levinson (1983, pp. 73–78) distinguishes between *linguistic tense* (L-tenses) and *metalinguistic tense* (M-tense). By L-tense he means what is usually referred to as grammatical tense in a particular language; by M-tense, he means a semantic or deictic category of tense, which indicates the temporal location of an event relative to the coding time (CT) and/or receiving time (RT) of the utterance. (Levinson points out that, in the canonical situation of utterance, RT and CT are assumed to be identical, an assumption called *deictic simultaneity.*) In an M-tense system, we distinguish the temporal location of events in relation to CT: *past* refers to events prior to CT, *present* to events spanning CT, *future* to events succeeding CT, *pluperfect* to events prior to *past* events (which are themselves prior to CT) and so on. M-tenses are important in separating the deictic features of L-tenses from their modal and aspectual features. For example, in English, L-future tenses always contain a modal element and in a decontextualized sentence it is difficult to know just what balance of "futurity" and "intentionality" is indicated by modals like *will, should* and *may* in examples like the following:

> I will never go hungry again.
> John should speak to her tomorrow.
> You may have visitors on Saturday morning.

Some languages like Chinese may not have morphological verb tenses markers (and so may lack L-tense in this sense) and yet, as Levinson says,

> ... we can confidently assume that there are no languages where part of an M-tense system is not realized somewhere in time-adverbials or the like, not to mention the implicit assumptions of M-present if no further specification is provided. (Levinson, 1983, p. 78)

Looking at examples of word problems from current British Columbia math textbooks, I found that determining M-tense in mathematical word problems is problematic. The difficulty is strongly linked to the lack of truth value in word problems—that is, their flouting of the Gricean maxim of quality. (For an account of the notion "flouting the Gricean maxim of quality," readers are referred to the entry on Gricean maxims in the appendix, which discusses H. P. Grice's concepts of implicature and cooperative principles in conversation.) Although several patterns of L-tense typically appear in word problems, their M-tense seems to remain consistent. For example, in many word problems the first two sentences use L-present and the third L-future:

> A truck **leaves** town at 10:00 a.m. travelling at 90 km/h. A car **leaves** town at 11:00 a.m. travelling at 110 km/h in the same direction as the truck. At about what time **will** the car **pass** the truck? (Alexander et al., 1989, p. 297)

> [A truck **leaves**: L- present
> A car **leaves**: L-present
> The car **will pass** the truck: L-future]

A second type uses L-past or L-present consistently in all three sentences.

> A ladder **is** unsafe if it **makes** an angle of less than 15° with a wall. A 10-m ladder **is leaned** against a wall, with the foot of the ladder 3 m from the wall. **Is** it safe ? (Ebos. Klassen & Zolis, 1990, p. 350)

> [A ladder **is**: L-present
> If it **makes**: L-present
> A ladder **is leaned**: L-present
> **Is** it: L-present]

> (This particular word problem is also interesting for its consistent use of passive, agentless sentences—there are no people in it.)

A great number of anomalies can be found which combine L-tenses in a self-contradictory way, that is, in a way that contra-

dicts the usual use of L-tense in English, where the statements are assumed to have truth value and the event is assumed to take place in a stable deictic relationship to
time (CT):

> Each elephant at the Young Elephant Training Centre in Pang-ha, Thailand, **eats** about 250 kg of vegetation in a day. How much **would** 43 elephants **eat** in 1 day? 1 week? (Alexander et al., 1989, p. 35)

> [Each elephant **eats**: L-present
> 43 elephants **would eat**: L-future.
> If we accepted the truth of the first statement (and it certainly sounds convincing, since we're given the name and location of the Elephant Training Centre), we would expect "How much **do** 43 elephants **eat**" in the second sentence.]

I think that the most sensible interpretation of the unstable temporal, locational and personal deixis in these word problems is to interpret all of the above as **M-tenseless** and **non-deictic** (Levinson uses this analysis on such sentences as "Two and two is four" and "Iguanas eat ants," for example (Levinson, 1983, p. 77)), but having **conditional** or **subjunctive aspect**. That is to say, the word problems do not actually point to a person ("Jake", "Jerry" or "you"), place ("the Young Elephant Training Centre in Pang-ha, Thailand") or time (before, during or after CT). Since these are not real places, people or situations, there is no absolute need for logical consistency in the use of L-tense (and L-tense is often used in ways that would be considered self-contradictory in standard expository English prose). Rather, word problems propose hypothetical situations with certain given conditions and ask for hypothetical answers. Most word problems could be rewritten in the form: "Suppose that (some certain situation A existed). If (conditions B, C, D, ... held), then (what would be the answer to E)?"

The very inconsistency and seeming arbitrariness of L-tense

choices in word problems points not only to their M-tenseless and non-deictic nature but also to an implicit "understanding" between writer and reader that these supposed situations do not have truth value and that the writers' intentions and the readers' task are something other than to communicate and solve true problems. (Otherwise the meaning of these problems in terms of a true situation would be very difficult to decipher.) This lack of truth value can be otherwise expressed as "flouting the Gricean maxim of quality ."

Flouting the Gricean Maxim of Quality

It is my contention a feature of the word-problem genre is a consistent flouting of the Gricean maxim of quality, which is to say that, as a genre, word problems have no truth value. This feature is intimately linked with, or perhaps a result of, their deictic indeterminacy. Time deixis, as shown through metalinguistic verb tense, has no referent. Personal deixis and place deixis (that is, the correspondence between the names of persons or places and their referents) have no truth value or are irrelevant. And yet the standardized form of the genre demands that declarative statements be made about these non-existent people, places and times. Such statements may be seen to be flouting the maxim of quality (which can be stated briefly as "do not say what you believe to be false").

An example from a math textbook currently in use in British Columbia:

> Every year Stella rents a craft table at a local fun fair and sells the sweaters she has been making all year at home. She has a deal for anyone who buys more than one sweater. She reduces the price of each additional sweater by 10% of the price of the previous sweater that the person bought. Elizabeth bought 5 sweaters an paid $45.93 for the fifth sweater. How much did the first sweater cost? (Ebos, Klassen & Zolis, 1990, p. 72)

The above could be reworded as follows without changing its

truth value (although it would be a rather odd-looking word problem, highlighting as it does one of the implicit features of the genre):

> Every year (but it has never happened), Stella (there is no Stella) rents a craft table at a local fun fair (which does not exist). She has a deal for anyone who buys more than one sweater (we know this to be false). She reduces the price of each additional sweater (and there are no sweaters) by 10% of the price of the previous sweater that the person bought (and there are no people, or sweaters, or prices) ...

The hypothetical nature of word problems can be understood here although it does not appear in the literal meaning of most examples of the genre. Again, Lave (1992) writes that "word problems are about aspects of only hypothetical experience and essentially never about real situations." (p. 78) This point is brought home in the cases where word problems seem to be referring to places, objects or people known to exist, as in the following:

> A rock dropped from the top of the Leaning Tower of Pisa falls 6 m from the base of the tower. If the height of the tower is 59 m, at what angle does it lean from the vertical ? (Ebos, Klassen & Zolis, 1990, p. 354)

The tricky part of the story problem above is the "if" (my emphasis). Certainly the Tower of Pisa has been measured. Why use the conditional form here? Is it intended to indicate that the vertical height of the tower is not stable? (This may be true—it was recently closed to visitors because increases in its "lean" had made it dangerous.) Or is it a way of subtly indicating that the referent for the words "the Leaning Tower of Pisa" is not the actual structure in northern Italy but a hypothetical tower, or stick, or line segment, whose height could be set at any value (say, 59 m) and whose slope could be calculated using the given numbers and the Pythagorean Theorem? Again, the writer of the problem seems to be taking pains to say, "Here is a story, ignore this story."

Tradition: "I Did Them and My Kids Should Do Them Too"

All this leads me to the question of the purposes of word problems as a genre. They are currently used as exercises for practicing algorithms, but such practice could certainly be achieved without the use of (throwaway) stories. The claim that word problems are for practicing real-life problem solving skills is a weak one, considering that their stories are hypothetical, their referential value is nonexistent and unlike real-life situational problems, no extraneous information may be introduced. Nonetheless, they have a long and continuous tradition in mathematics education and that tradition does seem to matter. Pinder (1987) makes a heartfelt case from a teacher's point of view for the non-practicality of word problems while acknowledging the strong pull of their tradition for the parent of one of her students. She discusses the following well-known word problem still current in textbooks, which dates back at least to medieval Europe and probably to Roman times:

> A basin can be filled by three taps: the first fills it in sixteen hours, the second in twelve hours and the third in eight hours. How long will it take to fill it when all are going together, if at the same time the basin is being drained by a pipe which can empty it in six hours?
> —problem collected by Alcuin of York (circa 790 A.D.) as paraphrased in F.P. Sylvestre's *Traité d'arithmétique*, Rouen, 1818 (Plane, 1990, p. 69)

> A water tank has two taps, A and B. Line A on the graph shows how the tank drains if only tap A is open. Line B shows how the tank drains if only tap B is open.
> a) How long does it take to drain if only tap A is open?
> b) How long does it take to drain if only tap B is open?
> c) Use the graph to find out how long it would take to drain the tank if both taps were open.
> —Kelly, Alexander & Atkinson, 1987b, p. 213

Pinder writes of the father of one of her students who complained that his child wasn't being taught problems like the one above (which he had studied in school). She writes:

> On reflection I realized how very stupid it was to create a problem, to be
> worked out by manipulating symbols, about a situation which no one in
> their right mind would ever create. The problem was that if one filled a
> bath, pulled out the plug and left the taps running, how one could find
> how long it would take the bath to empty. My question was: what did it
> matter anyway? What possible *use* would the answer be? Could it be
> that one might need to know whether the bath might overflow and cause
> a flood? But if so, why not just turn off the taps? But perhaps they were
> stuck. In that case surely it would be more useful for the children to learn
> how to turn off the water and how to locate the stopcock. All in all, a
> pretty useless problem for children to work on; so why was that father
> worried that his child was not going to have to solve it? (pp. 74–75)

Word Problems as Parables?

I earlier discounted the idea of word problems as a fictional
genre, citing their paucity of plot, character, human relationship,
dramatic tension, and so on. But what about Pimm's (1995, p.
161) suggestion that word problems be viewed as parables? In approaching this metaphor, I found both supporting and contradictory evidence in modern literary and theological theory that dealt
with parable in other contexts.

A number of writers acknowledged the non-deictic nature of
parable, a feature which we have seen in the word-problem genre.
Miller (1990) writes that

> all works of literature are parabolic, "thrown beside" their real
> meaning. They tell one story but call forth something else.... "Parable" is
> one name for this large-scale indirection characteristic of literary
> language, indeed of language generally. (p. ix)

In an essay on "Parable and Performative in the Gospels and
in Modern Literature", he writes:

> Etymologically the word [parable] means "thrown beside" [...] it
> suggests that parable is a mode of figurative language which is the
> indirect indication, at a distance, of something that cannot be described

directly, in literal language. [...] Secular parable is language thrown out that creates a meaning hovering there in thin air, a meaning based only on the language itself and in our confidence in it. The categories of truth and falsehood, knowledge and ignorance, do not properly apply to it. (pp. 135–139)

There is certainly the element of the indescribable involved in mathematical concepts, particularly those that deal with infinity or with entities that exist perhaps only as mental images and not in "this imperfect world" (an infinite straight line, a perfect circle, a point which has no part). Yet wouldn't the linguistic terms for these mathematical concepts (line, circle, point) be sufficiently "parabolic" deictic terms for these referents? Nonetheless, there is some appeal in the idea of story as a kind of homely way to refer to the indescribable, in the same way that religious parable speaks of spiritual matters in homely rather than theological terms. Miller's reference to the irrelevance of truth value for parables certainly could be seen to relate to the word-problem genre as well. Still, I am somewhat dissatisfied with Miller's fairly vague, general definitions; if the term parable can be taken to refer to all of language and literature and practically everything, what is its meaning?

Franz Kafka (1961), in his book *Parables and Paradoxes*, briefly introduces his definition of parable:

Many complain that the words of the wise are always mere parables and of no use in daily life, which is the only life we have. When the sage says: "Go over," he does not mean that we should cross to some actual place, which we could do anyhow if the labour were worth it; he means some fabulous yonder, something unknown to us, something too that he cannot designate more precisely and therefore cannot help us here in the very least. All these parables really set out to say merely that the incomprehensible is incomprehensible and we know that already. But the cares we have to struggle with every day: that is a different matter. (p. 11)

Again, we can find resonance in the metaphor of word problem as parable and Kafka's description could be read as the complaint of those like Pinder, who value real-life problem solving over the obscure references of word problems. I'm sure many perplexed mathematics students believe that "all these word problems really set out to say merely that the incomprehensible is incomprehensible and we know that already." But word problems differ from Kafka's parables in an important way—they stress the use of a correct method in order to arrive at a correct answer, while Kafka's wise one cannot suggest any course of action or any expressible goal. The illocutionary force of a word problem is an instruction to "Do this," "Solve this"; Kafka's storyteller is by no means so concrete or directive.

Oden (1978), in his preface to a collection of Kierkegaard's parables, asks:

> Why do we read Kierkegaard's parables and why do they merit philosophical attention? Is it because they are like maddening puzzles daring some attempted solution? Is it because the problems they address drive to the depths of ordinary human experience? Or are they mere entertainment, revealing the comic side of human pretenses—subtle poetry, with virtually inexhaustible levels of meaning? Wherever the weight of the answer is to fall, anyone who lives with these parables for a while experiences both their power and their beauty. Soon you realize that it is not you who are interpreting the parable but the parable that is interpreting you. (Oden, 1978, p. ix)

Here I think the metaphor of word problem as parable begins to break down. Although word problems may be puzzles and maddening ones at that, they do not dare but require solution—that is a large part of their force as speech acts. And I think it would be hard to argue that word problems, used as they are in our schools as "disposable" exercises, could be lived with over time and seen to have inexhaustible levels of meaning, particularly poetic meaning about the depths of human experience. Nonetheless, there is the question of the durability of certain word problems, some of which appear to have been taught to scholars for centuries or millennia. Perhaps there is something elemental or common to human experience in these, if we could find it, although perhaps their endurance simply speaks for the incredible conservatism of mathematical tradition.

Finally, in his book on the parables of Flannery O'Connor, May (1976) quotes Via, a modern hermeneutic scholar:

> For Via the parable in the narrow sense is "a freely invented story told with a series of verbs in the past tense" (e.g., the Prodigal Son, the Talents, the Unjust Steward). It is not concerned with the typical but with "making the particular credible and probable." In the parable strictly conceived as fiction, "we have a story which is analogous to, which points to but is not identical with, a situation or world of thought outside of the story." (p. 14)

Thus far, the analogy with word problems holds up fairly well. The non-deictic use of verb tense, the concern with the credibility of particulars in a form that both does and doesn't refer to the particulars of the everyday world, all seem parallel. On the other hand, May writes:

> Inasmuch as the parable in a narrow sense thrives on the drama of human encounter as a figurative expression of the drama between God and man, it uses ordinary human language, rather than specifically theological terms, to mediate the ultimate reaches of reality to man. Reflecting the historical situation of their author, the parables proclaim what it means to exist in a boundary situation, how the eschatological crisis occurs within the confines of everyday existence. (p. 15)

Although word problems do reflect the historical situations of their authors, I think it would be stretching the metaphor rather far to claim that they "mediate the ultimate reaches of reality to man," that they involve eschatological crisis, or that they express the drama between human beings and God.

Perhaps in the exercise of viewing word problems as parables, we will be able to see word problems in a different way that will allow us to generate new ways of using them. I suggest, too, that delineating the boundaries of the word-problem genre can allow us to play with those boundaries in interesting ways. In any case, I do feel that it is important to think in new ways about the nature and purposes of word problems, about their inherent oddness and contradictions and about our rationale for using them in school mathematics programs rather than simply, unthinkingly visiting them upon future generations of schoolchildren.

Chapter 4
Word Problems and Intentions:
A Study

In Chapter 3, I presented an analysis of mathematical word problems from the perspective of linguistics and literary criticism. In the next three chapters, I report on a small-scale empirical study undertaken to generate responses to this analysis.

Methodology

In the previous chapter, I briefly introduced ideas about intentions—teachers' and textbook writers' pedagogic intentions in presenting word problems to students (word problems' illocutionary force); what students make of their teachers' intentions (students' uptake of that illocutionary force); and the things students do when presented with word problems (word problems' perlocutionary force).

In planning the empirical component of this study, I wanted to "try on" ideas about intentions and referentiality with thoughtful practitioners and students in the field. I wanted to inquire into pedagogic intentionality around word problems as they are used in educational practice and to see what thoughtful teachers and students made of the anomalies I saw as inherent in the word-problem genre.

My purpose in these interviews was not to *describe* the use of word problems in classroom practice but to find out about the perceived purposes of their use by those who create and present word problems to mathematics students and about what students make of being presented with such problems. I was particularly interested in ways that the illocutionary force coded within word problems in their cultural context might contradict the stated intentions of educators and the ways that students might "read off" or take up on intentions coded in the genre that teachers or text-book writers might not be aware of.

The methodology used in this study was qualitative, focusing on questions which emerged with increasing specificity over the course of the research, following Lincoln and Guba (1985). In such research, the researcher is the instrument. As a person sensitized to the issues at stake, I have recorded the way that things "struck me" over the course of the study.

Throughout the collection and analysis of data, I looked for two kinds of examples to emerge—*illustrative examples*, which relate directly to the textual analysis presented in Chapter 3 (and either support or contradict that analysis) and *generative examples*, which generate ideas not previously considered. This is the strength of qualitative research methods—that new hypotheses may emerge in the course of field experience, even as previously formulated hypotheses are tested.

Where possible, I aimed for oblique questioning techniques in an attempt to minimize the possibility of interviewees inventing opinions not previously held merely to satisfy the interviewer's direct questions. One method of oblique questioning that I used was successfully established as a research method by Schoenfeld (1985) in his work on mathematical problem-solving heuristics. It is a "think-aloud" method, where interviewees are asked to think out loud while engaged in a problem-solving task and the results are recorded (in this case, on audiotape and later transcribed). Where possible, I used this method with pairs or small groups of students, since some degree of "thinking aloud" is necessary when working with a partner or partners and is thus more natural than in a one-on-one interview.

In my selection of subjects and research sites, I took an opportunistic sample of teachers, curriculum materials writers and students from elementary, secondary and post-secondary institutions in Vancouver and Burnaby, British Columbia. I also interviewed two prominent mathematics educators, Pearla Nesher, of the University of Haifa, who is well known in international mathematics education circles for her semantic and syntactic analyses of mathematical word problems and David Robitaille of the University of British Columbia, who has carried out a number of international comparative studies in mathematics and science education achievement. In my reports of interviews with Nesher and Robitaille and with curriculum writer Dave Lidstone, the interviewees requested that their real names be used. In reporting on interviews with writers, teachers and students, the names of those interviewed have been replaced by pseudonyms to protect their anonymity.

In choosing people to interview, I sought out those who seemed to be the most interesting and worth looking at rather than an "average" population that it would be safe to generalize from. In this study, "the most interesting" is interpreted as the most knowledgeable, thoughtful and innovative practitioners of mathematics education that I could find.

Intentions vs. Constraints

As rhetorician Jamieson (1975) showed in a well-known paper on rhetorical genre, generic forms carry with them a history of culturally and linguistically coded intentions. The use of a generic form may bring with it intentions that are not exactly the same as those of the current writer or speaker. Jamieson gives the example of a papal encyclical which borrows from the rhetorical forms of a Roman imperial edict. She argues that contemporary readers interpret a papal encyclical and its Latin prose style as pompous, turgid and overbearing in part because the encyclical is written like a message from the Roman emperor.

Word problems, as a very old generic form, also carry with them intentions which act as a rhetorical constraint to the intentions of contemporary mathematics educators. Rifts between the conscious, stated intentions of educators and the illocutionary force of word problems are often focused on anomalies of reference or deixis. In particular word problems display an unusual, non-referential use of verb tense as well as nouns which refer only tangentially to lived experience of people, place and things and more directly to a world of mathematical forms and structures, where structurally isomorphic objects, persons and places are interchangeable. Contemporary writers and teachers may consciously intend to refer to their students' lived lives, to "real-life" situations when they offer word problems to students. The genre itself may constrain or subvert these conscious intentions through intentions carried by its very generic form—the intention not to refer to the "things" talked about in the word problem in a straightforward, literal way but in a coded and ambiguous way to both those real-life things and, more strongly, to the "things" or objects of a world of mathematical concepts different from the world of everyday experience.

For this reason, educators' stated and often sincere intentions with regard to the use of word problems may be read as a justification or alibi, in terms acceptable within our culture, for a form which doesn't necessarily fit that culture. The generic form carries with it intentions that are throwbacks to cultural norms of mathematical education from earlier times and other places. Word problems are interesting as artifacts in the archaeology of mathematics education, sedimented as they are with meanings from other worlds. They are much more than simple straightforward applications of mathematics to real life.

Interviewing: Getting Beyond the Obvious Answer

Researchers conducting qualitative studies often note that new questions and methods emerge as a result of engagement over time in the field of study. Over the course of my study, I was surprised to discover that my own interviewing techniques had to change if the interviews were to yield non-trivial results.

In my previous experience as an interviewer (partly in the context of journalism, film, television and radio production), I had learned an interviewing style which consisted largely of "keeping quiet and letting the other person do the talking." This kind of documentary or journalistic interview style works well when the interviewee has been chosen as an expert or spokesperson on a particular subject and the aim is to get as much uninterrupted film footage as possible with that person talking to camera to allow for the greatest flexibility in editing.

In this study, however, the "expertise" was in the process of being formed in a "third space" between me as interviewer and the interviewees. The interviewees (teachers, students, curriculum writers) knew the contingencies of their own day-to-day practices within mathematics education and the ways that idealized intentions were changed by the power struggles at play in educational systems. I knew some of the internal contradictions inherent in a genre widely used in their educational practices and I knew that these coded, linguistic contradictions might in themselves undermine stated pedagogical intentions.

Our interviews took on the character of teachable moments. For my part, when I found an interviewee giving an easy and somewhat superficial response (like the often-repeated assertion at an early stage in the interviews that word problems were simply mathematics applied to real life), I would offer a contradictory example from a familiar source, usually the writer's, teacher's or student's own textbook. Then I would re-ask the initial question and this time get a response that showed greater depth, originality and uncertainty. Sometimes several "re-asks" and counterexamples were needed to get both interviewer and interviewee past the level of the superficial answers and received wisdom. It was at this point in the interviews that unexpected, surprising and thought-provoking results typically emerged from the interviews.

The idea of the "teachable moment" relates both to me and those I interviewed. For my part, I found myself taking a didactic role in the early stages of the interviews, trying to establish a common vocabulary and common ground in the discussion, "teaching" the interviewees what I had learned so far about word problems. This went very much against the grain for the filmmaker in me. In a film context, I would not contradict, however gently, the ideas the interviewees had come in with, since that would constitute the crime of asking leading questions. Yet in the context of this study, if I didn't work to move the interviews beyond predictable initial responses, I wouldn't be taking advantage of the reason I had chosen these people as subjects for the study—that is, their thoughtfulness and enthusiasm to engage with and generate new ideas in mathematics education. Without a firm but gentle nudge onto new ground, a nudge very much from the world of teaching rather than journalism, the interviewees and I would simply be restating our preconceptions. By finding new ground in an interactive conversation about word problems, a space was created where the interviewees could, in turn, teach me and lead me beyond my preconceptions.

Nonetheless, I am left with a number of uneasy questions about the nature of interviewing. If the interviewer is carrying out a genuinely qualitative inquiry, rather than simply trying to find evidence for accepting or rejecting a pre-formed hypothesis, then what is an acceptable mode of conversation in the interview? If the study is not ethnographic, attempting to observe and describe "the other," but conceptual, attempting to consult and collaborate with others on matters of mutual interest, then to what extent should the interviewer's voice and ideas be present? These questions are not the focus of the present study but merit further consideration on their own.

Chapter 5
Teachers' and Curriculum Writers' Intentions

Curriculum Writers and Critics

In this portion of my account of the small-scale empirical study, I report on interviews with four people who write and critique mathematics curriculum materials: Dave Lidstone, a college mathematics instructor and curriculum writer; "Hannah Krauss", a writer of primary school math textbooks as well as a teacher and curriculum consultant; David Robitaille, a Canadian university mathematics educator who has carried out several large-scale international comparative mathematics education studies using word problems; and Pearla Nesher, an Israeli university mathematics educator, whose semantic and syntactic studies of word problems are well-known in the field of math education.

Dave Lidstone teaches calculus and other math courses to college students, many of whom plan to transfer later to university. Although he uses a textbook series for some of his curriculum materials, he also writes many of the word problems and other curriculum resources for his courses. Lidstone is very active and well respected in the Canadian mathematics education community and has served on the executive of CMESG, the Canadian Mathematics Education Study Group. He has recently completed his Master's degree in mathematics education.

Lidstone and I had talked previously about my work on the analysis of word problems and he had attended a conference session I had given a year before about anomalies of reference in word problems. He wrote to me after the conference, expressing concern about how to make word problems better and offered examples of word problems he had written for one of his calculus courses.

When I asked him why he wrote and assigned word problems in his calculus classes, Lidstone raised the question of whether students were being asked to abstract the math that was inherently "there" in a word problem story or whether they were to project the mathematics onto an intrinsically non-mathematical situation. Although he spoke about both projecting mathematics and finding mathematics in real-life situations, in his own work as a curriculum writer he seemed to be "seeing calculus" everywhere as if differentiability, for example, were an inherent quality in certain kinds of situations.

Lidstone had sent me a calculus word problem he had written about the acceleration of a model rocket and he indicated that it was based on a scene that he had observed—a family launching a model rocket in a park near his house. I asked him whether his starting point in writing the problem was the real-life situation (observing people in the park launching a rocket) or whether he had started with an algorithm or a symbolic idea that he wanted to flesh out. Or did he start from several angles at once? His reply showed the priority of the antecedent word-problem genre and the textbook organization of mathematical concepts over the exigencies of the real-life experience in itself:

> DL: I will offer that there is certainly a variety of factors that come in right from the outset [in the writing of a word problem]. And I think that again the biggest one is experience. So not only experience with well-established structure for word problems, not only that. But things like, well with respect to the rocket problem, the experience that our differential calculus courses typically have linear motion as an application. But typically the problems are so abstract that—there are certain particles moving along certain lines that really have no real context to them—so that they indeed are not word problems but are really just strictly exercises. There's no abstraction, there's none of the aspect of taking some sort of real-world situation and taking the mathematical presentation, the mathematical ideas and seeing them in this real-world situation.
>
> And so I guess as I go through life I look for those real-world situations as screens on which to project math. And in this case these people were

playing with a model rocket, and, gee, I could do the timing that was necessary and I think I had some sort of sense that this lends itself—I knew
what type of ideas this situation lends itself to. I was very familiar with
abstract problems from textbooks that addressed exactly the same abstract mathematical issues. And so it was easy enough to describe it.

Lidstone, with his focus on his work as a teacher and writer of
initial calculus course curriculum, had come to see the world
through "calculus eyes." With the course's conceptual
organization and an inventory of typical calculus problems in
mind, he attended to the world of his daily experience with the
idea of finding further, better examples of that curriculum, better
instantiations of those problems:

SG: From the point of view of someone who writes curriculum material,
writes word problems or find them or creates them—do you start seeing
the world as, do you find yourself focusing your attention on things that
are possible examples of the things that you're teaching?

DL: Yes. Very much so … And yes, I do have the theoretical library
stored there and then look for examples as they manifest themselves. And
that's probably the factor that I use most in creating word problems.

His aim in writing calculus word problems and assigning them
to his students is not simply that the students use a correct solution method or arrive at a correct answer. Rather, he hopes that
the students will begin to do as he does—to see the world with
"calculus eyes":

SG: I'm also trying to think about what you hope your students will take
away with them once they've solved that particular problem or a whole
bunch of problems. Do you want them to start looking at the world in
that way too?

DL: Certainly. Yes. I would like them to be able to see mathematics in or
project mathematics onto situations around them. So I do try to focus on
things that might be more immediate than many word problems that you
would see in typical textbooks.… The model rocket problem appears in

textbooks but in an abstract way. "A certain particle moves in a straight line with a particular acceleration." What I try to do is say, well look, that abstract thing, we can see it here too, in the backyard.

Although Lidstone wrote word problems as ways of "fleshing out" abstract mathematical ideas and saw the resulting stories as "nonsensical" to some degree, he emphasized that the word-problem stories were required to have some very specific points of contact with the "real world" of our experience. He told the story of one of his students who viewed word problems as a completely nonsensical coding of abstract mathematical ideas and refused or failed to make contact with one of the specific "real world" conditions that Lidstone had meant to be part of the word problem about the model rocket's rate of acceleration. As a result, the student arrived at an unacceptable solution to the problem:

> DL: There was an interesting interaction with one student about this problem. This is a student who was trained in mathematics in Russia. This student is much more comfortable with formal mathematics and symbolic manipulations; many of the things most of our North American students struggle with, he's very adept at. I should add that this young fellow had no language difficulties. His command of the English language was very good. But he was quite dumbfounded by this problem because he didn't bring a real-world context to it at all. He took a traditional, completely nonsensical, abstract approach to it. So the solution that he offered was quite irrational ....

> SG: Is it that he had never seen people with a model rocket?

> DL: No, he thought it was completely irrelevant. His solution made an assumption that the rocket wouldn't come down in spite of wording that obliquely suggests that it will. And again I'll say obliquely because it's something that the students need to bring to the modeling. The engine provides an acceleration, and then the rocket travels under the influence of gravity. The inference they need to make is that the gravity will provide a deceleration and hence tend to bring the rocket back down.
> So his solution assumed that that was gravity from somewhere else—that it just went forever and ever and ever. But he's the only student I've had who ignored that context, who in essence assumed it was nonsense. All

of my other students with that problem have recognized that this is not
nonsense. This is significant to what we have to do here.

The paradox raised here is an important one—that solvers of
word problems must attend to a few contextual features and discard many others. For example, it would not be considered relevant in the solution of the model rocket problem to attend to information about the color or sound of the rocket, the names and
relationships of the people firing the rocket, their reasons for
choosing to fire off a model rocket in the park, or the weather
conditions during the launch. These and many other features of
the situation might be important to a real-life participant in the
event, but the word problem is not *about* launching a model rocket
in all its complexity—it is about sketching a curve, remembering a
formula, differentiating an equation. It is about math and only certain types of questions about the real-life situation are permissible
(for example, what is the magnitude of the force of gravity?) The
students are given no explicit instructions about what to attend to
and what to ignore, but they will have seen several mathematically
similar solved word problems in their textbook that give object
lessons in how to solve "this type" of problem. The word problem
itself may also have, as Lidstone says, "obliquely worded" hints
as to which aspects of the story situation are to be considered relevant. And once the student has solved a great many of a certain
type of word problem, the weight of a large number of repeated
examples is meant to provide a repertoire of experiences (within
the world of mathematics schooling) from which generalizations
about word problem solving may tacitly be drawn. It is interesting
that this pedagogy, a pedagogy of tacit generalization over the
course of many examples, seems to have changed little since the
time of the word problems of the Babylonian scribal schools
(about which more in Chapter 7).

It was interesting that, although Lidstone was in the habit of
"seeing the world with calculus eyes" and could cite many examples from his daily experience that exemplified the concepts in-

troduced in the initial calculus courses, he found it much harder to find examples for other, more elementary mathematical concepts not included in his own teaching. Later in the interview, I asked Lidstone to "think aloud" as he devised word problems on the spot that would correspond to particular symbolically stated math problems from the elementary and secondary school curriculum. I had deliberately chosen problems that I thought would be difficult to exemplify and that was one reason why Lidstone found these word problems difficult to write. But he also found that the numbers I had offered him were not "nice numbers"—in other words, they were not numbers that would typically occur in the contexts he had devised for the word problems. Again, although the point of contact with lived experience seemed slight, it was important to Lidstone to "get the numbers right," so that the word problem stories would not seem completely nonsensical.

> DL: 4.79 plus 108.324 [the arithmetic problem from which I asked him to write a word problem]. This is something that is perhaps a little closer to my experience, mostly with my daughter [in helping her with her elementary school homework]. And yet the .324 eliminates the natural context of money. So what would jump into my mind would be some sort of measurement problem in some context, in a laboratory or some such thing. Now I would also then look for some sort of instrument that measured to thousandths of an inch. I focus on thousandths of an inch rather than focus on metric because the instruments with which I am most familiar that uses thousandths of an inch or measurements to three decimal places are feeler gauges for engine repair. But what is unfortunate there and would make the problem difficult is with the calling of tolerance on the low end; you wouldn't be concerned with numbers on the high end, the 108. So I would really search for some kind of meaningful context here.

> The thing that now comes most to mind is monetary exchange. 'Cause this is where you could have these two scales coming in, 108 dollars, 32 and a half cents. Eventually you'd ignore the point four but that would be a significant figure on the way to arriving at an exchange. I will offer that this probably came to mind, probably surfaced because I just got back from a week's holiday south of the border, sorting out exchange rates, exactly these kinds of figures would come up. Offhand I can't think of too

many situations where those kinds of magnitudes would simultaneously be considered—hundreds and thousandths. That might be more a measure of my inexperience with the world ....

[Looking at another question:] Five ninths equals *x* over a hundred and eight.... What immediately popped into mind were any number of problems that in essence had a context that was nonsense. "Five ninths of the marbles in this bowl are red. There are 108 marbles in this bowl. How many of them are red?" Where in essence the context really is [...] nonsense. I can't help but think that if I didn't gravitate to that because of the experience I've had with textbooks, where that's a common practice, I might find this easier to address with a word problem if either I had more experience with things that might have 108 as a unit or if this were some other number that were standard as a unit. Say 60 as in seconds, 120 as in a fairly standard angle, something like that. I would find it easier to provide a—

SG: Why don't you write some different numbers for a similar kind of question and then tell me the word problem that you would write, one that would be more sensible or less nonsensical?

DL: Well I guess that some of the units that would come into play would be 360 degrees for a complete revolution or 180 degrees for a straight angle, twelve for months of the year, 24 for hours of the day. And I think it might be easier to work with any such numbers. That said, here's one. "A contractor estimates that it will take 108 person hours to complete a job.... " It's so silly, it's so stupid! I was going to go on to something like, "Partway through the job, the contractor is fired. The customer only pays him five ninths of the contract. How much time was put in on the job?" Something like that. It's a curious situation to be placed into, to look for context for equivalent fractions...

It's curious that I find myself being at a loss for ready word problems, largely because these are not concepts that I teach day to day, so they're not things that I look around the world and look for examples for.

SG: That's really interesting because they're very elementary concepts, yet it's so hard to find those examples...

DL: Well, or to have a catalogue of anything but fairly standard types of problems.

Lidstone's response here is notable on two counts. For one, although he had the habit of "seeing calculus everywhere" and finding many sources of calculus word problems in his daily experience, he did not also "see ratio everywhere" or "see decimal fractions everywhere" or at least had difficulty seeing the ratios and decimal fractions I had offered him (5/9 and 108.324). Presumably, the ability to see the world as a source of examples for a particular branch of mathematics requires focus on that branch of mathematics. Although the secondary school mathematics curriculum was certainly familiar and elementary to Lidstone, he was not seeing the world in terms of those concepts because he was not engaged in teaching them. Similarly, Lidstone's students, who would have been studying three or four other courses in nonmathematical disciplines and perhaps working part-time at a nonmathematical job at the same time they were taking his calculus course, would be unlikely to see the world "through calculus eyes" as Lidstone wished, simply because they were unlikely to be focused on calculus to the extent Lidstone was.

The other notable theme in Lidstone's response is an impulse to write word problems that are as sensible and true to life as possible. He is concerned that the numbers used be reasonable within the context of the word problem story and that the stories and numbers should make sense, should *mean* something in an everyday, non-mathematical world. In Chapter 7, I will show that this has not been of great concern to most writers of word problems throughout their long history, beginning with the Babylonians, and I would argue that word problems' intrinsic non-referentiality mitigates against students considering them sensible or true in any case.

Other contemporary curriculum writers have also expressed concern about word problems' nonsensical nature and have made an effort to work out guidelines for writers to make word problems unassailably sensible and true to life. One interesting example of this kind of effort comes from Marks (1994).

Marks is concerned that secondary school students "perceive

word problems as questions that no real person would be caught asking" (p. 610). He gives the example of the familiar "age problem," a category of word problems used in introductory algebra courses and popular in books of recreational mathematics:

> "Five years from now Mary will be twice as old as her sister; how old are the girls now?" The student wonders, "Don't these girls know how old they are? If not, where could such information about their future relative ages possibly have come from? And who cares?" Every such answerable question drives a wedge between the student and the problem; insert enough wedges and the entire subject falls apart like a split log. (p. 610)

Marks goes on to give other examples of "un-sensible" word problems and describes ways of revising them so that the teacher could provide an answer to any potential student question about the trueness to life or practical meaning of the story.

What Marks and Lidstone do not account for is the idea that word problems as a genre are not *about* everyday life, even though one or two contingencies of the story situation may be considered relevant to solving a particular word problem. Students become acculturated to the use of word problems and learn that they are not stories about everyday, commonsense situations. Marks acknowledges that few secondary school students will voice objections about the nonsensical nature of word problems but he worries that "teaching word problems becomes a nightmare when students start asking such questions out loud" (p. 611). He suggests that writing more true to life word problems will be beneficial in reducing teachers' embarrassment at having to justify the inclusion of word problems in the curriculum: "The teacher's success in making word problems more sensible can be measured by the gradual decrease in tension he or she feels during such discussions" (p. 611). I doubt, though, whether an individual teacher's efforts to justify the use of word problems by writing only "sensible" ones can effectively counter the weight of thousand of years of teaching/riddling/storytelling tradition which is so much embedded in the problems' very form.

"Hannah Krauss", a writer of primary school mathematics textbooks, has recently completed her doctorate in mathematics education, focusing on young children's emerging concepts of number. She taught and worked as a consultant in elementary schools for many years and is currently teaching mathematics methods courses to preservice teachers in university.

In Krauss' work as a textbook writer and teacher with young children, she rarely uses printed word problems, concentrating instead on different kinds of modeling, counting, grouping and notation activities that relate to things familiar to children. (For example, she structures one activity around finding patterns in the numbers of letters and their distribution in children's first and last names.)

Krauss sees generic word problems as contrived and unrealistic and the writing of word problems as an exercise in "clothing" mathematical ideas in situations.

> HK: It's attempting to take the mathematical and tack it somehow, have it hooked onto something that might be at least familiar even if it's not interesting or relevant.

> SG: It seems to me that people writing these problems start with an addition question and an idea of what type of addition question they're going to do, and then everything's added on afterwards.

> HK: Dress it up—right. I think so. Absolutely.

And yet, when I asked her for an example of a mathematical modeling question that was a real-life problem (as opposed to the contrived situations used in word problems), Krauss immediately suggested a very old, determinedly impractical word problem. (This problem can be seen as a version of the "100 Birds" problem, which Tropfke (1980, pp. 613-615) credits to Chang Ch'iu-Chien in ancient China and later to Mahavira in India, Abu Kamil in the Islamic world and Alcuin in medieval Europe.)

HK: [There are] chickens and cows in a farm and there's a fence and you can see so many feet and you know how many animals there are alto-gether—how many [of each animal] would there be? Children doing that would not start thinking algebraically about what would make sense to add up to the right number of legs. They would be drawing chickens and cows and counting their feet. … By and large they are drawn to the more real applications of what would it look like.

SG: Mind you, that's not a very real application, because you'd never do that! Is it a puzzle; is it a riddle?

HK: What, the problem? It's just a way to get kids to think about different combinations of what could add up to things and putting it in a way that they need to model it to find out—draw it or think about it in different ways.

Although Krauss designs modeling activities using familiar, often concrete objects that are familiar to children, she recognizes that even these activities have been devised as ways to embody mathematics and may veer sharply away from practical, everyday uses of those objects. She tells the story of one child who couldn't or wouldn't do a regrouping activity she proposed because it was nonsensical:

HK: I was doing a sharing problem with kids … and I had these little bagged sets of objects to share … There were sort of birthday party kinds of things in packages with a number on them and so we'd say, "Oh, here are eight party hats. If you and I were going to share them, how many would we each get?" So if they've got [the idea that four is] half of eight, or four and four is eight, they can just let go the party hat issue of "Why would you want four party hats?"

Well, the youngest boy, Sam, who always touched his fingers to his nose as he counted, had trouble with the bag of twelve red spoons. I chose that because the [number] twelve was [written] really big on [the package], and they were sort of party looking spoons and so on. And I said, "If you and I were going to share these spoons, how many would we each get?" And we'd talked about fair shares, and he'd done it with the blocks. "Well, we only need one spoon each," he said. And I said, "You're right.

If we're going to eat with them, you're right. But if it was just pretend—if you were going to set one table and I was going to set the other, how many would we each get?" "No, no," he said, "we only need one spoon each, so we'd just give the rest of them to somebody else." So I guess Sam was very context bound and literal about what was going on there and the whole context of the problem meant a lot to him and it did have to make sense. But for most kids the sharing of twelve spoons wasn't such a problem.

SG: But in almost every other part of their life, the context would be extremely important. If they're learning to set the table at home and if there are six spoons in the drawer and four people, they can't give each person a spoon and a half!

HK: He was the only one who had a problem with that.... So then I said, "Do you want to use blocks instead of spoons? Should we do it with twelve blocks? "And then he was quite happy with that, sharing twelve blocks.

Although it's clear that Krauss is working to find sensible, real-life, familiar situations for mathematical modeling, she runs into the same kind of problem that troubled Marks—that is, students refusing to engage with the mathematics of a problem because its story is nonsensical in everyday terms. Even in Krauss' modeling activities, which depart from the linguistic formalism of generic word problems, the words and objects point to a world of mathematical concepts, not a world of everyday, lived experiences. Students who are "context bound" and "literal," who have not learned or accepted the ambiguity of reference inherent in mathematical word problems (or "practical" problems they are antecedent to) may be unable or unwilling to take up the parabolic meaning of the problems because their straightforward, literal meaning does not make sense.

David Robitaille, a mathematics educator at the University of British Columbia, has been co-author of three large-scale international comparative studies of schoolchildren's competency in mathematics and science, most recently, the 1997 Third

International Mathematics and Science Study (TIMSS). These studies have included a large number of word problems. I asked Robitaille why such problems were included in the TIMSS survey. He acknowledged that word problems were quite different from "real-life" practical problems but, like a number of other university mathematics educators I spoke to, attributed this difference to a scaling-down of real problems to match students' limited mathematics knowledge:

> SG: Isn't it the case that if a student knows too much about the real-life situation, they may be unable to do the word problem the way they're supposed to? They'll take too many contingencies into consideration, or they'll want to do the problem the way you would in real life.

> DR: Oh sure. All of the average speed problems for example. What would life be like without those? [laughs] That's very much the case. The problem is simplified so as to make it within the mathematical competency of kids.

Robitaille seemed to see word problems as good motivators to get kids involved in solving mathematical problems—again, an idea I heard several times, mostly from elementary and secondary school teachers:

> DR: At some level, you want the problem to engage students. You want them to say, "At least this is interesting enough that I want to find the answer."

I asked if there were any problems involved in the translation of word problems across languages and cultures. Robitaille could only recall the following example:

> DR: The item as I recall asked kids—it was a multiple-choice item—if they knew the word "carnivore." And in the Norwegian version of it that was piloted—apparently they don't use the word "carnivore," they have a Norwegian word. So the question, if you had translated it into English, said, "What do you call a meat-eating animal?" and one of the answers was, "A meat-eating animal"! You sort of defeat the purpose of

the whole exercise. It wasn't a very good item to begin with, fortunately, but it didn't survive. So quite a few items got thrown out on things like that.

He referred me to a comparative international study of mathematics textbooks written as part of the TIMSS study by Howson (1995). Howson, in a comparison of selected English, French, Japanese, Dutch, Norwegian, Spanish, Swiss and American textbooks, indicated that "the percentage of word problems to be found in texts has increased, in some cases enormously" (p. 58) and that Augustus De Morgan, in 1831, had noted the discrepancy between "real-life" problem-solving methods and those required by word problems in mathematics education. (For example, De Morgan wrote, people would never actually find the value of a horse by solving a pair of simultaneous linear equations.) Other than this, there was no further mention of word problems in an international, intercultural context.

Pearla Nesher is a mathematics educator from the University of Haifa in Israel. She is prominent in the mathematics education community for her work in the language of mathematics education and has written about the syntax and semantics of mathematical word problems.

I asked Nesher about educators' intentions in including word problems in mathematics curriculum and about the non-referential quality of such problems:

> SG: There's a particular word problem I thought we could focus on.... It's something like this: "A rock dropped from the Leaning Tower of Pisa falls 6 m from its base. If the tower is 59 m in height, what is the angle of its lean?" ... Is this really a question about the Leaning Tower of Pisa?
>
> PN: No, not at all. It's a question about triangles. It's probably in the framework of trigonometry. It's just that somebody thinks it will bring a real problem from real life... It's good to have a diagonal line like that but it's really no [real-]world [situation]. You are not allowed to drop stones from the top of the Tower!

My favorite example [of an unrealistic word problem] came from a teacher who asked the children to write a problem to fit the open sentence, "Two plus seven equals nine." Make a story. It was second graders. One child said, "Mommy has two irons. She buys nine more irons. How many irons will she have?" Very practical question!

Nesher asserted that the mathematical structure takes a position of primacy in the writing of word problems. Although curriculum materials writers might intend to use word problems to teach mathematical modeling, the arbitrary and unrealistic stories of word problems mitigate against students learning to model real situations mathematically:

PN: A situation by itself does not imply any mathematical structure. We put structure on it by the way we look at it. Now deep in our understanding, mathematics is useful because we can use models to gain information that we wouldn't know from just looking at the [real-life situation]... The whole issue of word problems is of finding the right models for the right situation. And I don't know if we convey this notion to the kids when we teach them. We bring our artificial cases. We use awkward language which we would not usually use.

I talked with her about the idea that word problems were more closely related to parable than to real-life problem situations in terms of their reference. She agreed that students soon learned to read word problems as non-referential and learned to throw away the stories in order to look for the mathematics that they were expected to do:

PN: Here is a story which is not about what it's meant to be about... You say something and you mean something else. And that's what the kids get very easily. In the word problems you are right. Here you mentioned the Pisa Tower, but you really don't mean the Pisa Tower. You could use any other thing. And the kids get exactly the notion that what you are asking them is about the computation. They don't care about the words. We can bring whatever context we want, interesting for them or not. In a minute they will understand that this is not it.

Nesher's suggestion to improve this situation (similar to an approach suggested in Smith, 1988) was to use more real-life problem solving to encourage students to apply mathematics to actual situations in their lives and particularly in their schools:

> PN: I think that maybe if we work on more complicated situations, fewer situations, not ten simple, unimportant word problems but one more complex situation and there are examples—If you ask a child to calculate how much the teacher has to ask to bring for a party, if it's a real problem—how much should we ask each student to pay for that party? OK, that's complicated. Why should we pay that much or that little? How much should each one in the classroom bring for the end-of-the-year party? There are a lot of pragmatic questions which are not part of mathematics, but the child has to know that the class will have to make choices...

> Even for small kids, we have to look for problems which are more complicated in terms that we don't make all the decisions for the kids and they have to understand what's involved in modeling and that we have to make mathematics. I don't know if I have enough problems yet which are interesting enough but I know what we should collect—problems that are not simple, that the child must use mathematics in order to know, and where he will find that the situation is not artificial.

University Mathematics Teachers

I interviewed two university mathematics teachers at Simon Fraser University about their pedagogic intentions in assigning word problems to students in their undergraduate courses. (I have used pseudonyms in all the reports on teachers and students that follow, to protect their identities.) "Mohammed Ibrahim" is a mathematician who has taught introductory calculus courses at SFU for several years. "Alan Robbins" is a statistician who has taught both the introductory statistics courses and introductory calculus.

In all my interviews with teachers, I tried to use examples from the textbooks and other curricular materials they used in their teaching to prompt a further consideration of intentions around mathematical word problems. In my interview with Ibrahim I used examples from *Calculus: Second Edition* (Stewart, 1991). In my interview with Robbins, I used *Probability and Statistics for Engineering and the Sciences* (Devore, 1991).

Robbins candidly admitted to the influence of a strongly conservative mathematics teaching tradition and to simple expediency in teachers' decisions to use word problems in their mathematics classes.

> SG: Why give word problems to students?
>
> AR: Well I guess the first thing is that every book that's published has got them in so there's a certain amount of just going along without thinking about the problem at all, just giving, not the word problem but thinking about why there are word problems. You just accept it.... There's a certain amount of just going along with it, period.

He also indicated that the disguising of mathematics within the stories of word problems could serve what he saw as a useful purpose—to complicate an otherwise overly simplified elementary mathematics curriculum.

> AR: You can't give, in this type of course here, strictly mathematical types of problems because they're too hard generally for the students to do. So you take just some simple little concepts there that might be very simple mathematically but you hide them in the word problem. They have to go and find them in the word problem and then they see, "Well, gee, it's really not that hard to solve mathematically." So that's probably the reason that they're done in my course anyways.

Robbins sees the word problems in his statistics textbook as far removed from the reality of his daily experience working as a consulting statistician who advises scientists and other professionals on experimental design. Although the textbook he has chosen uses examples taken from a wide range of professional journals (including, for example, *Water Resources Bulletin, Photogrammetric Engineering and Remote Sensing, Equine Veterinary Journal, Journal of Solar Energy Engineering, Journal of Consumer*

Affairs, and *Textile Research Journal*), he feels that the word problems included in the textbook are far from being true to life.
Instead, Robbins says that his students are being asked to make a
model of a model:

> AR:[The textbook's writers] have probably taken real situations and of-
> ten they quote from journals, from other journals that they've looked up
> and they condense it down; they take the data out and condense the
> whole article into two or three sentences just giving a part of the bottom
> line of it and then there's a little bit of mathematics to do.

> So I guess there's the real problem and then there's the textbook problem
> which has really squished it down and then students have to take that
> and try to go one more step and translate it into mathematics and try and
> solve the problem related to the original problem but with this math-
> ematical model....

> So I guess we could say that a word problem is a model of a real problem
> and then the mathematics is a model of the modeled problem (laughs). So
> there's a couple of steps of modeling. And how far from reality you get
> would vary from problem to problem, I would imagine.

Robbins was very clear that, for him, word problems were
"about" the mathematics they were meant to hide and not about
the stories themselves:

> SG: In these story problems, do the stories matter?

> AR: No, I don't think so. Not in these cases here. I mean, I could take a
> concept two-thirds of the way through the book, say, a concept that
> we're trying to illustrate—testing hypotheses, for example—and I could
> come up with examples in computer science, biology, education, English,
> you know. "Was this newly-discovered sonnet really written by
> Shakespeare or not?" That sort of stuff.

Robbins focused on the parabolic, parable-like deictic nature
of mathematical word problems to the point where he seemed not
to notice the stories at all before discarding them in favor of a

hidden mathematical relationship. For example, I showed him the following word problem taken from the statistics textbook he had chosen for his class. This story in this particular problem had troubled me when I was a statistics student several years before:

> The article "Rate of Stuttering Adaptation Under Two Electro-Shock Conditions" (*Behavior Research Therapy*, 1967, pp. 49–54) gave adaptation scores for three different treatments: (1) no shock, (2) shock following each stuttered word and (3) shock during each moment of stuttering. These treatments were used on each of 18 stutterers.
> a. Summary statistics include
> $x_{1.} = 905, x_{2.} = 913, x_{3.} = 936, x_{..} = 2754,$
> $\sum_j x_{.j}^2 = 430,295, and \sum \sum x_{ij}^2 = 143,930$
>
> Construct the ANOVA table and test at level .05 to see whether true average adaptation score depends on the treatment given.
> b. Judging from the F ratio for subjects (factor B), do you think that blocking on subjects was effective in this experiment? Explain. (Devore, 1991, p. 413)

SG: What do you make of that?

AR: Well, horrifying, isn't it? Horrifying.

SG: Why is it horrifying?

AR: Maybe it's too concise. I could sit down and construct the analysis of variance table from it and do the tests and everything, but it just seems—That's the kind of thing that a mathematician would be interested in. You want that conciseness down.... But it doesn't relate it very much to the stuttering experiment. You've kind of really lost contact with the stuttering experiment there. So that was the original one. The scientist has set up the experiment, decided what the treatments are going to be—shock, no shock or different variations on the shock. They would have done the appropriate randomization. And then they've gathered all these stats here, and they've just given you a very concise compilation of the data there. And it's not very interesting. I would agree, it's not very interesting.

SG: The thing that got to me was the idea of people who stuttered being

given electroshocks. I couldn't really get past that...
AR: Well for me, reading this here, I just kind of skip over that. I just think—it just doesn't even register with me. All I'm saying to myself is, OK, there's an experiment going on here and there's three different treatments—one's no shock and I'm thinking, OK, there's your control group right there. And then there's two other shocks. I'm thinking of those. I'm not thinking at all in terms of what's happened to these people! I'm thinking of just two different treatment groups. So I must admit, my mind's a long ways from the experiment. I just look at the data, analyze the data, and see if there's a difference there. But certainly that aspect didn't even cross my mind. But you couldn't get past that part of it, eh?

SG: Well, it seemed like torture to me...

AR: It's interesting though that you're thinking of that aspect of it and that's completely—I'm oblivious to it.

Robbins' colleague, Ibrahim, who had grown up in Iran, *did* see the implication of torture in the "stutterers" story problem:

MI: I don't know what the state of mind was of the person who wrote this! Maybe he was teaching math in prison? This problem is a joke, of course?

Ibrahim offered three different reasons for using word problems in mathematics teaching—to prepare students to be mentally receptive to mathematics, to offer familiar images for abstract concepts and to justify mathematics to students as a practical subject.

First, in considering word problems as mental preparation for learning mathematics, Ibrahim focused on the story-telling aspect of word problems. He considered story-telling as an informal, mentally relaxing, sociable activity that could both interest and in some way disarm students, making them more receptive to the more abstract mathematics that would follow:

SG: Why use story problems in mathematics teaching?

> MI: You set up your mathematical problems in the form of stories to pre-
> pare the mind of the student. You have to teach smoothly. The stories give
> the student *time* to think, to be absorbed by mind ... I'm beginning to think
> that when you tell students stories, it takes a bit of pressure off their
> minds.

Related to the idea of storytelling as a source of mental relax-
ation, Ibrahim emphasized the homeliness and familiarity of story
images as a *way in* to the "otherworldly" world of mathematics. In
his emphasis on the use of narrative form and familiar imagery to
point to an abstract world of mathematical concepts and relationships, Ibrahim approached the idea of parables, which use familiar stories to point to an other world of invisible, intangible moral
and religious precepts. He insisted that mathematics not be perceived by students as "hocus-pocus." He argued that removing a
sense of mystery and inaccessibility from mathematics instruction
would make the subject more comfortable and familiar for students. "Telling them everything" (like a seasoned magician who
lets a novice in on the tricks of the trade) should allow students to
feel like insiders and demystify mathematics for them:

> MI: The other answer to this question is that you are trying to use other
> tools to reach the students. You're going to ask for help from some other
> area. A story helps you to explain the mathematical stuff. Why does it
> help? Because mathematics is a different world, a strange world for a
> student. You want to make it less strange, more familiar to students. You
> want to create an environment where the student relaxes his mind. You
> want to assure them it is not hocus-pocus.

> SG: Tell me more about magic and hocus-pocus.

> MI: It can look like hocus-pocus if you teach math very fast, very ab-
> stractly. It can become hocus-pocus very soon! I think the whole idea of
> mathematics education is to avoid that situation.

> Magic is something everyone agrees they don't understand. But in math
> you want them to understand. You want to *show* them how to do that

magic. You have to tell them everything!

Although Ibrahim acknowledged that word problems were far from being "real-life" problems, he saw them in terms of *justifying* mathematics to students. This kind of justification is a half-truth at best since, as Ibrahim indicates, the mathematician or mathematics teacher is not really interested in the contingencies and complications of experienced situations nor in the plausibility of solving an actual problem using mathematical means. For the mathematician, mathematics is goal enough and if the story problem serves as sufficient justification to convince students to engage with the mathematics, then it has served its purpose:

> MI: We want to show them applications of math. Students ask, "What is this math good for?" It's a kind of *justification* for the reasons they have to learn math. I'd say these are applications.
>
> In word problems, teachers are making stories to teach mathematics. With many of these stories, you could ask, "How can this happen? Would this really happen? How many times does this actually happen to anybody?" But still, they are good practice. Students learn theory only through examples. otherwise, nothing makes sense...
>
> (Referring to a word problem from the textbook he uses, about maximizing revenues from an apartment building) These problems are made up by mathematicians and teachers. I really don't know whether in real life a manager is going to take a pencil and pen and work this out. Most of the time real-life problems are more complicated than these are.
>
> For example in physics word problems, there are a lot of other factors you forget about—you have to assume this or that to be true. Writers of word problems want to make them ideal problems for the framework of theory they are teaching.

Ibrahim noted with some irritation that real-life problems from the sciences, for example, were anything but elementary if considered in their true complexity and that their solution would thus not allow them to serve as exemplars of particular elementary mathematical methods or ideas. For Ibrahim, the pedagogical needs of mathematics teachers and students in the math class took precedence over actually solving problems from physical science or other real-world domains.

> MI: In the calculus textbook quite a few of the word problems deal with physics. As a math teacher, I don't know a lot of physics myself and I don't want to bother to go into the study of physics!

> Besides, with these problems, if you consider other factors, suddenly they become *research* problems! For example, some of the calculus problems talk about throwing a ball up in the air. In these problems, we are not meant to consider air resistance but only gravity. I'm not teaching physics, I'm teaching calculus!

In Ibrahim's interview, a clear view emerged of the centrality of mathematics as a deictic object for mathematics teachers. It was clear as well that, in his role as a mathematics teacher, he desired that mathematics become such a deictic object for his students and that he was willing to lead his students toward this end through the warmly familiar medium of storytelling and even through some small degree of trickery (through the use of story problems to justify mathematics). What mattered to him as a teacher was that students accept mathematics as a "thing" to be referred to, as a world that could be *seen through* the transparency of everyday images. Mathematical word problems could then serve multiple and simultaneous purposes—to "warm" students to mathematics through the comfortable, relaxing mode of storytelling, to provide familiar images for the abstract concepts of mathematics and to convince students to accept mathematics as a central "world" through its presumably practical applications.

Secondary and Elementary School Mathematics Teachers

In contrast, the elementary and secondary school teachers I interviewed viewed mathematical problem solving as ideally offering a particular instance of general problem-solving strategies that could apply to other fields as well. Their aims, as they articulated them, did not place mathematics in a central deictic role. Rather, the general process of problem solving was (or ought to be) the focus. Through mathematical word problems, they felt they could offer students a chance to appreciate multiple approaches and strategies to all kinds of problem-solving. Where Ibrahim wanted students to "see through" the images of the story problems to the particular mathematics they were meant to learn, "Laura Bertrand," "Carol McKay" and "Marianne Reed" wanted their students to keep a stronger sense of the situated, contextualized meanings of the word-problem stories and to focus on using particular problem-solving strategies to solve them. At the same time, they did want their students to learn the particular mathematical ideas addressed in a textbook chapter through these same word problems and this posed some degree of pedagogical conflict for these teachers.

"Laura Bertrand" is a Grade 5/6 teacher in an elementary school in a working-class neighborhood of Burnaby, a suburb of Vancouver, British Columbia. She coaches several sports teams and often uses sports images and references in her conversation. "Carol McKay" is a secondary school mathematics teacher and math department head in a school in that same neighborhood. "Marianne Reed" is an elementary school teacher and principal in another school in Burnaby. She takes a special interest in improving elementary math education and often gives math workshops to teachers in the district and to student teachers at Simon Fraser University.

Bertrand's keen enthusiasm for mathematical puzzles was clearly evident in my conversations with her. (On first meeting, we took a half-hour walk around the school neighborhood, exchanging favorite math puzzles.) She said that her primary reason for presenting mathematical word problems to her students was to encourage them to take a similar pleasure in problems as puzzles.

SG: What do you want the students to learn from word problems?

LB: The thought process. Different ways of solving problems. There's not always one way. To think creatively. There are strategies that can be taught in the solving of a word problem and that's the reason for doing it: to teach them different strategies and teach them an enjoyment of a puzzle, of an unknown.

Bertrand used word problems from puzzle books, wrote her own problems and assigned her students problem-writing tasks as well as using word problems from textbooks. She said that her pedagogic aim was to emphasize the process of problem solving and to teach students multiple problem-solving strategies rather than to focus on mathematical algorithms that would generate a single "right answer":

SG: When you have the kids write their own problems, do you give them some arithmetic to start from and then ask them to write a problem around that?

LB: Not usually. It's open-ended, where they can choose a problem, or they must have an end point, where I'll say, "Your answer must be 1997." They can use different methodology and different terminology within their own problem. That's one of the ways that I do it... Kids like that. They enjoy the unknown, figuring it out and then seeing if they can't figure it out... it's strategies you're learning. And the strategies apply across the board. They don't just apply to math. And that's what I like about them.

SG: Can you give an example?

LB: Well, I think "guess and test". If sometimes trying to do something doesn't work the first time, "guess and test." Try another way of doing it. That can work in shooting a basketball. It can work in making a cake. Say you guessed wrong; you put in the wrong amount—why? Those things—they can assist you in real-life situations. And just the joy of figuring something out, the accomplishment of figuring something out you didn't think you could. That's really important to me, too.

Other people avoid problem solving like the plague. It's always the end product they're worried about. They're not worried about the process. And I'm worried about the process more than the end product. But in most things I do—I'm worried that you played the game well, not whether we won or lost. That's my philosophy on lots of things. So that's why. It carries through into my math as well.

In the same interview, however, Bertrand said that the skill most needed by students was the skill of converting word problems to math algorithms—that is, the skill of removing the decorative "dressing" of story from a word problem and uncovering the specific mathematical techniques and pertinent data intended by the problem writer:

LB: I think that's the biggest problem the kids have got. " I don't know what to do here. What do I do here? What do I use here?" At all levels, that's what they want to know. How to convert [word problems] back and forth.

SG: How do you want them to do that conversion?

LB: It's getting the information. It's gleaning the information as to what is going to answer the problem. So, being able to pull out the important points. What's important here? What numbers are important here? What amounts are important here? What's the process that they're asking you to give? Those are the things that are important within the word problems, what numbers and what the numbers mean in relation to one another and what you're trying to achieve in the word problem...

SG: How do they find out which information *is* important?

LB: Well, that can be a taught skill. That's a skill you can teach kids—to read and find what's being asked, or what kind of questions mean what kind of things and what kind of information means what kind of things. That's a skill you teach them in a word problem. It's the reason for doing it.

Bertrand's intention to teach students flexible, transferable, generic problem-solving strategies is clearly at odds with the idea of teaching them to find "the process they're asking you to give."

This "translation" or conversion skill does not allow for multiple strategies and approaches or for open-ended problems. It is clearly aimed at teaching one particular technique which will lead to a correct answer.

There is an evident conflict in Bertrand's statements about her intentions in using word problems as part of her math teaching. The force of tradition and traditional expectations within mathematics teaching (in the form of the demand that students be proficient at translating word problems from story to algorithm and back again) competes with the demand that students become flexible and creative problem solvers, an expectation voiced in the NCTM (1989) Standards documents, in numerous calls from business for a more adaptable, "problem-solving" workforce and many other contemporary sources. While it seemed clear to me that Bertrand preferred to frame word problems as open-ended puzzles whose solution involved a pleasurable element of play, she also felt an obligation to offer them in the more traditional school context, as exemplars of particular taught mathematical techniques which could be extracted or uncovered by removing the guise of story. I was left wondering whether Bertrand's students were able to tell which skill they were expected to demonstrate in a given lesson—the skill of flexible problem solving or the skill of translation.

In a similar way, McKay saw two conflicting intentions at play around word problems in the secondary mathematics curriculum. Throughout my interview with her, McKay expressed frustration at not being able to work towards the pedagogic goals that she valued. She implied that curriculum and time pressures in her dual role as mathematics teacher and department head prevented her from teaching the way she would like to. (In fact, as an illustration of the busy lives of teachers, much of our interview was conducted in near-whispers as McKay simultaneously supervised a number of students writing a noon-hour test in her classroom. Similarly, my interview with Bertrand was conducted in low voices in her classroom while her class did silent reading, since our lunchtime appointment had been taken up with an emergency staff meeting.)

McKay made a distinction between her ideal use of word problems (as real-life, contextualized problems admitting a variety of strategies and approaches) and her actual use of them (as traditional end-of-textbook-chapter "hard problems" that must be translated to the algorithm taught in the chapter and solved correctly). She expressed a sense of guilt at being forced by circumstances and time pressure to fall back on the traditional approach:

> CM: Would you like me to comment on what I do this year, or what I would *like* to do this year? Are you interested in the reality or the philosophical view?

> SG: Both.

> CM: OK. Well I'll start with the reality. The reality this year is that I've tended to use word problems basically as they occur in the context of the topics I've been teaching. We haven't looked at word problems as a mathematical idea in its own right, where there are strategies to be learned and approaches to take. We've just done them as an extension of a concept, to take a concept and put it into context. Which is a valid reason but there's more to it than that if we're using problem solving. But that's really been it—to illustrate the context of a particular idea... It's what I end up doing. I end up teaching the mathematical idea more than I do the problem-solving skills.

Like Bertrand, McKay has the conflicting intentions of teaching generic, flexible problem-solving strategies (which she sees as an ideal reason to teach with word problems) and of teaching the traditional "translation" from story to math, which she sees as a fallback to a less-desirable teaching intention:

> SG: This is from the *Mathematics 9* book (Kelly, Alexander & Atkinson, 1987a), page 27, number 3.

> Pietro had twenty problems for homework. His mother paid him 25 cents for each one he solved and deducted 35 cents for each one he couldn't solve. Pietro earned 80 cents. How many problems was he able to solve?

When your students get a problem like that, what do you want them to do with it?

CM: Well, it would depend on why I was presenting them that problem in the first place… In the grade 9 course one of the strategies we spent a long time on is using algebra. So it may be how to develop an algebraic method for solving this problem. That would be the more usual way to teach—to show how you can solve this problem algebraically. That's not my ideal but it is the reality of what I do.

When I asked McKay why she thought the story "dressing" was part of word problems, she too invoked the idea of "translation" from natural language to mathematics:

SG: So what would be the difference between giving the kids this problem in story form about Pietro and his mother and his homework or giving it to them in a purely algebraic form, say a system of linear equations with $25x$ minus $35y$ equals 80 ?

CM: Well, if we did that, then that part of the problem is solved for them because you've given them the x's. The idea is that part of this problem is to be able to *translate* a problem that's in one language, which is English, into another language, which is mathematical and that involves x and y. So that's part of the process if the methodology that you want them to learn is algebraic … Part of that methodology is to be able to translate, literally, from one language to another, from the English language to a universal, mathematical symbolic language.

McKay acknowledged traditional algebraic "translation" techniques of solving word problems as valid but as only one of many possible valuable approaches to problem solving. She suggested that practical pressures of her teaching situation obliged her to emphasize this approach to the exclusion of others and that she was unsatisfied with her own teaching for this reason. Like Bertrand, she would have preferred to use word problems as a means for teaching multiple strategies in problem solving rather than focusing solely on translation to a single correct algorithm.

McKay also indicated that she would be willing to entertain a more contextualized, possibly less mathematical problem-solving approach rather than stripping away "extraneous" elements of the story as is traditional in teaching word problems. I read her the following story, reported recently from an English elementary school:

> It was a lesson under the heading of "ratio and proportion" and the teacher told me that she wanted to approach the mathematical concepts in a practical way. So she offered the following question: "Somebody is going to have his room painted. From the painter's samples he chooses an orange color which is composed of two tins of red paint and one-and-a-half tins of yellow paint per square metre. The walls of his room measure 48 square metres altogether. How many tins of red and yellow are needed to paint the room the same orange as on the sample?" The problem seemed quite clear and pupils started to calculate using proportional relationships. But there was one boy who said, "My father is a painter and so I know that, if we just do it by calculating, the color of the room will not look like the sample. We cannot calculate as we did, it is a wrong method!" In my imagination I foresaw a fascinating discussion starting about the use of simplified mathematical models in social practice and their limited value in more complex problems (here the intensifying effect of the reflection of light) but the teacher answered: "Sorry, my dear, we are doing ratio and proportion." (Keitel, 1989, p. 7)

> SG: What are these problems really about? Do you read them as a story, or "read through" the story?

> CM: In the context of that situation, not having been there but assuming it's as it happened, I'm surprised the teacher wasn't a bit more flexible. That's very exciting to me that that person would bring that point of view in. Even if, in the end, you end up teaching the ratio, which is as she said was the mathematical purpose, the mathematical idea—
> So the purpose to her then probably wasn't problem solving, it was how to solve a ratio. If her purpose was problem solving, then to me it's very exciting that this person said, "Hey, let's take a look at this, this is a much bigger thing," and all that kind of thing. You can do lots with it. But she wasn't teaching problem solving. She was teaching that particular ratio.

In a similar way, Reed, in her work with elementary school students and with in-service and preservice teachers, placed far greater value on teaching generic problem-solving strategies than on teaching "translation" of word problems to a single correct algorithm:

> MR: I fear that people will see problems again as word problems, which are just drilling practice on algorithms. That is, putting meaning to those isolated facts. So now we put some words around it. We use this problem to practice a skill that we've been learning. Word problems are the lowest level....
>
> I don't think a lot of people see it that way. They don't think about problem solving that way. They see a problem in the textbook and say, "OK, I'm doing problem solving." But I think problem solving is far more complex than that.

For Reed, pattern problems and mathematical puzzles are distinctly different from word problems, the "lowest level." Reed sees word problems as admitting only one correct approach and one correct translation (that is, to the algorithm that is the focus of the current lesson). She sees such a single correct approach as allowing for no alternate strategies. It is a "make-or-break" situation for the student—either the student knows how to make the right translation or not. If not, there is no recourse, no alternate means for the student to move toward a solution. On the other hand, Reed's preferred mode of problem solving is to offer problems where data must be organized in some way in order to reveal patterns which can be used to solve the problem:

> MR: I think there are different kinds of problems. There are story problems, like "Three birds sat on the telephone line and two more birds came. How many birds do we have altogether?" Those are story problems based on specific operations—addition, subtraction, multiplication, division.
>
> I think there are also problems that require strategies to solve. That means you look for a pattern, you set up tables, you do all sorts of things. Then there are the puzzle problems. And I think they are three very different kinds of problems but I think they're all lumped together and I don't think they're taught carefully as strategies.
>
> I will spend a whole term on pattern problems and we'll really exam-

ine problems for patterns, so it becomes a strategy that kids will use. I was never taught to do that in school. I was taught to read the problem and solve it. I had no ways to attack the problem. And I think that's where the [Gary Larson "Far Side"] cartoons [about math anxiety around word problems] come from and I think that's where the anxiety comes from.

Like Bertrand, Reed values students' learning of problem-solving processes over the production of right answers:

MR: I try to tell kids now, "It doesn't matter if you get the right answer. That's not what I'm looking for. What I'm looking for is your thinking on how you've approached the problem." I have kids do a lot of writing in problem-solving math. They must rewrite the problem in their own words. That's to demonstrate that they understand what the problem is asking. And then they must write their steps as they do it and show pictures and diagrams of what they're doing. As they work through a problem they've got to show how their thinking is going. So when I mark their problem, that's the meat—the thinking is the meat. To get the right answer, that's fine, but that's worth only one point.

Although actual teaching practices are not accessible from the interview data, Reed gave indications that she instructed students in specifically mathematical problem-solving processes, particularly in terms of arranging data in the form of tables and graphs and looking for numerical patterns. Bertrand, on the other hand, mentioned problem-solving processes like "guess and check" that may be useful both in mathematical and generic problem-solving situations. McKay indicated that, although her current practice consists solely of mathematical "translations" of word problems, ideally she would like to teach problem-solving in a more generic context, where both mathematical and non-mathematical ways of solving could come into play.

If it is possible to draw any general conclusions from this small sampling of teachers' and curriculum writers' stated intentions around the use of word problems in mathematics classes, it is the following.

In my sample, it seemed that the closer that teacher was to elementary school work, the more the teacher's pedagogic focus was on teaching generic problem-solving strategies, both mathematical and non-mathematical, through mathematical word problems. Problems were allowed to remain relatively highly contextualized. A stripping away of the story context and subsequent "translation" to an abstracted mathematical algorithm, although sometimes acknowledged as useful, were seen at best as only one of many possible problem-solving strategies. Those closest to elementary teaching who also had a strong connection with university mathematics education (Krauss and Reed) emphasized strategies based on numerical pattern but nonetheless allowed for multiple approaches to a problem.

In contrast, the closer the teachers were to the higher levels of tertiary education, the more their pedagogic focus was on "the mathematics" of the lesson as an object and the more they were likely to expect students to see through the word problem stories to abstract mathematical structures. For the university and college mathematics instructors I interviewed, word-problem stories might serve to motivate or relax students, to persuade them of the efficacy of mathematics or to give them useful mental imagery. For these instructors, though, the pedagogic reason for using word problems was always to focus students attention, *parabolically* (as with parables), on an abstract mathematical structure or a particular mathematical method. In one case (Robbins), the mathematical methods took precedence over the story to the point where the story disappeared or perhaps never succeeded in engaging the instructor's conscious attention. Robbins was so much attuned to "seeing through the story" that, for him, the story had become entirely transparent. He was not at all aware of the invisible story he was "seeing through" so clearly.

In this scheme of pedagogic intentions, with a focus in elementary education on generic problem solving and in tertiary education on abstract mathematical structures, it is not surprising that the secondary teacher I interviewed was the instructor who

seemed to face the greatest internal conflict about her own pedagogic intentions. Sensing collegial pressures (and setting her own
internal standards) to teach both generic problem-solving skills
and abstract wholly mathematical objects through mathematical
word problems and working under stressful time pressures,
McKay repeatedly apologized that she had failed to meet her own
pedagogic ideals.

Chapter 6
How Students Read
Their Teachers' Intentions

Why do students think that they are offered word problems to work on in mathematics class? How do students read their teachers' (and textbook writers') intentions around the word problems presented in mathematics courses?

Leaving aside statements which could be read two ways because of their ambiguous wording, language philosopher H. P. Grice found that a flouting of unspoken but understood co-operative principles by one or another speaker could account for unintended readings of an utterance. Thus, in Gricean analysis of conversation, interlocutors may frequently "read" a speaker's intentions in ways that were not intended by the original speaker. In linguistic pragmatics, cultural schemata which underlie an utterance may or may not be shared. (For example, saying that "the bride wore a scarlet wedding dress" may have different meanings in Western and Chinese cultural contexts. In Chinese culture, a red wedding dress symbolizes good luck and respect for tradition, while in Western cultures it might be taken to symbolize promiscuity and a flouting of tradition. In traditional Chinese culture, white garments symbolize mourning and are worn at a funeral, while in the West, a white wedding dress represents virginity and purity.) Closely related to unspoken cultural schemata are the cultural messages and implications carried by generic forms, implications carried by the genre itself and not necessarily available to the speaker.

I had the sense that the word-problem genre might carry meanings unintended by teachers and curriculum writers and that these coded intentions might be taken up by students who were offered word problems in their mathematics classes. Also, I suspected that students, whose interests and position within schooling systems differ from those of their teachers, might make sense of the practices of schooling in a different context and so read intentions different from those stated by their teachers in the word problems they were asked to solve.

To explore this line of thought, I interviewed groups of students at elementary, secondary and tertiary levels of education, from elementary school students to university undergraduates. Wherever possible, I tried to interview the students of the teachers I had interviewed. Table 1 shows a summary of the student groups interviewed, including the students' age and level of schooling, the location of their school, the name of their teacher (one of those whose interview was reported in the previous chapter) and the number of students in the group. Interviews typically lasted 45 minutes to an hour and were audiotaped and transcribed. All student names used are pseudonyms.

Of all the groups of students I interviewed, the students who offered the most varied, elaborated and well-thought-out rationales for the use of word problems in the mathematics curriculum were the university undergraduates. There are several possible explanations for this.

For one thing, these students were relatively mature both in terms of their mathematical sophistication and life experience. Many of the undergraduates had worked in several adult work settings, either in part-time and summer jobs, through co-op work experience programs, or through several years of work undertaken between high school graduation and university. In addition, many of these undergraduates' jobs involved applications of mathematics in fields like engineering, the sciences and business. While the student teachers interviewed had a similar degree of life experience and had worked at jobs, most of this bilingual group of French immersion teachers identified themselves as "language people, not math people," and several said that they were math phobic. The student teachers had not worked in areas of applied math and tended to focus on talking about difficulties in interpreting the wording of word problems rather than the mathematical intentions of curriculum writers and teachers.

Table 1: Students Interviewed

Student age	Level of schooling	School location	Teacher	Number in interview groups
10–12 years	Elementary (Grades 5/6)	Burnaby, BC	"Laura Bertrand"	2 groups of 3, 1 group of 2
13–15 years	Secondary (Grades 8/9)	Burnaby, BC	"Carol McKay"	2 groups of Grade 8 students (4 and 2 students respectively); 2 groups of Grade 9 students (3 and 5 students)
18–25 years	University undergraduate students	Burnaby, BC	"Mohammed Ibrahim," "Alan Robbins"	Calculus and statistics students: for each, 1 group of 3 and 1 single student;.
23–30 years	Preservice elementary French immersion teachers	Vancouver, BC	"Hannah Krauss"	1 group of 7 students

Undergraduate Mathematics and Statistics Students

The three undergraduate calculus students I spoke to as a group had all worked in mathematics-related jobs outside the university. When I first asked them why word problems featured so prominently in their calculus textbook, they were firm in their belief that these were real-life problems like those students would encounter on the job:

SG: I'm trying to understand from teachers' and students' and textbook writers' points of view why people think these things [word problems] are included in math education. Why are you presented with these things in your textbook?

Mike: Basically because it's the easiest to associate with real life.
Cyril: Yeah.

Antonia: Also when you're working, that's the type of problem you're going to get. A client's going to come in and say, "This is my problem." They're not going to say, "A equals B, C equals—." They're going to say, "I have a problem with something," and if you're an engineer, or no matter what, that's how it gets worded. And really, that's how business works. We have to learn to solve it that way.

SG: So are they practical problems? Are they applied? Are they ways of applying math to life?

Cyril: Yeah. I think so.

Antonia: And I think with all the talk these days about universities being full of theory and little use when you get out in the work world, I think they need to make—right from the start the word problems have to be more work applied. In the sense of where one day you might actually go, "Hah! I did a problem in first year calculus that was exactly like this!"

As counterexamples to the idea of word problems as practical applications of mathematics, I asked the students to read aloud the following several problems from their own calculus textbook:

> 33. A 160-lb man carries a 25-lb can of paint up a helical staircase that encircles a silo with a radius of 20 ft. If the silo is 90 ft high and the man makes exactly three complete revolutions, how much work is done by the man against gravity in climbing to the top?
> 34. Suppose there is a hole in the can of paint in Exercise 33 and 9 lb of paint leak steadily out of the can during the ascent. How much work is done? (Stewart, 1991, p. 866)

This pair of problems elicited quite a different response from the students, who saw this word problem situation as nonsensical and not an example of mathematics applied to the working world.

> SG: Is this an applied question?
> Antonia: Well, yeah, I guess, if he was a painter or [laughs] if they wanted to know—[laughs] I'm not sure why they would want to know ... I don't care whether a man walks up a staircase with paint, like, how much work it takes him. I mean, he either gets to the top or he doesn't. My first thought was, "He doesn't have to paint the stairs". [all laugh]

> Cyril: He might as well just go back down.

> Antonia: You know, he'll have a high dry cleaning bill and—[laughs] It's not interesting... I guess it's a personal thing, but as far as applied being for life, I mean, have you climbed a staircase recently with a can of paint?

> Mike: I think pretty much they just wanted to give you a question, and they needed to word it somehow. And they want to word each question differently. And basically they just tried to make it make sense in some way by giving you the different—circular and amount of time. It makes it a little bit more difficult... I don't think that particular question is relevant. It's just like giving you numbers except it's even making less sense, because who really cares how much work you do when you carry a can of paint upstairs? I don't know why anyone would actually want to find that out.

The students' comments here particularly interested me for their sharp about-face from ideas expressed just moments earlier. When confronted with particular word problems from their own course, the students decided that the problems were not necessarily applications of mathematics to real-life job situations and, in fact, did not make sense in terms of a lived context. Mike's comment that "they just wanted to give you a question and they needed to word it somehow" seemed particularly resonant with Lidstone's comments as a curriculum writer. Lidstone had said that he carried a "library" of typical calculus problems around in his head and looked for life situations onto which he could project the structures of those problems. Mike seemed to capture in brief

that idea of "a problem looking for words," a mathematical structure that curriculum writers wanted to present to students and
which must, for some reason, to be "bodied forth" in the words
and images of a story, whether an everyday story or a nonsensical
one.

Mike's response to the following problem, also taken from the
students' own textbook, showed a similar perception of the intentions of curriculum writers which seemed close to writers' own
previously quoted accounts of their task:

> If an arrow is shot upward on the moon with a velocity of 58 m/s, its
> height in meters after t seconds is given by $h = 58t - 0.83t^2$.
> a) Find the velocity of the arrow after 1 s.
> b) Find the velocity of the arrow when $t=a$.
> c) When will the arrow hit the moon?
> d) With what velocity will the arrow hit the moon? (Stewart, 1991, p.
> 103)

> Mike: With this question I don't see why—they pretty much had a couple
> of numbers, and they wanted you to figure it out. And so they just de-
> cided, "We want to make this simple so we don't want to have gravity in-
> volved in it, so we'll just say, OK, we're firing an arrow on the moon."
> It's not relevant anyway. I don't think they had a question, and then they
> decided to put numbers in. They had the numbers, and they decided to
> make a question to fit the numbers.

> SG: Why not just give the numbers?

> Mike: That would probably make it a lot simpler.

On the other hand, the same group of students responded
positively to the ring of real-life familiarity that gave the following
problem interest and relevance for them:

> The manager of a 100-unit apartment complex knows from experience
> that all units will be occupied if the rent is $400 per month. A market
> survey suggests that, on the average, one additional unit will remain va-
> cant for each $5 increase in rent. What rent should the manager charge to
> maximize the revenue? (Stewart, 1991, p. 242)

Mike: I don't know. I think that question's a lot better than the others because it's actually useful.

Cyril: Yeah.

Mike: You can actually incorporate that in real life. It makes more sense that way than firing an arrow on the moon or carrying a can of paint up a silo.

Antonia: Plus we rent, so you can understand the rental and I guess—instinctual information. You know, if you're thinking about a period of time, twelve months, things like that, it's automatic, more comfortable. Because by this point in university most people have had an experience of being renters if you like. So it just feels more familiar.

SG: So the story makes a difference? Does the story make a difference?

Antonia: Without having solved it—!

SG: Just your initial reaction.

Cyril: Yeah, yeah.

Mike: Yeah.

Bram, a classmate of these calculus students who was interviewed on a separate occasion, expressed a similar increased interest in word-problem stories that seemed to relate to his real-life situation:

Bram: I'd say that you don't look at problems that you're not interested in as hard as you do if you're interested in it. Like I know with myself, whenever there's word problems with golf or something where somebody's hitting a trajectory or whatever like that, then it's like, cool, I can sort of think about this. And then next time I'm out golfing I sort of think about that again. I've done that before.

Unlike his classmates, Bram did not express the opinion that word problem stories were simply examples of mathematics applied to practical, real-life situations. Instead, he talked about having the "mindset" of treating life situations with available mathematical methods:

> Bram: [reads] "A boat is pulled into a dock by a rope attached to the bow of the boat and passing through a pulley on the dock that is 1 m higher than the bow of the boat. If the rope is pulled in at a rate of 1 m/s how fast is the boat approaching the dock when it is 8 m from the dock?" (Stewart, 1991, p. 164)

> SG: Is this a practical problem?

> Bram: I don't think you're going to actually be calculating how fast the boat's going to come in if you're pulling it in... You're just going to pull and as it comes in you're just going to watch and see that it's coming in and you shouldn't pull as hard or something like that. But once you know how to do some of this kind of stuff, you just sort of get the mindset that you could calculate stuff like that if you have to.

For me, Bram's comment that "you just sort of get the mindset that you could calculate stuff like that if you have to" is very close to mathematics historian Jens Høyrup's comment about ancient Babylonian word problems—that they "appear to have been chosen... just because they *could be solved* by the methods at hand." (Høyrup, 1994, p. 7, discussed at length in Chapter 7 of this book).

Bram, like Mike, saw the textbook writer's intention as that of fleshing out a mathematical relationship with some kind of story. Bram generously took it on himself to try to imagine real-life situations in which he might encounter situations similar in their mathematical structure to those presented in a word problem, situations in which recalling the word problem from his calculus textbook might help to solve a practical problem in life:

> Bram [reads]: "A man starts walking north at 4 ft/s from a point P. Five minutes later a woman starts walking south at 5 ft/s from a point 500 ft due east of P. At what rate are they separating 15 min after the woman starts?" (Stewart, 1991, p. 164)

SG: Is this a practical question?

Bram: Well, I guess this could be practical, if you're in a scavenger hunt or a treasure hunt or something like that, or if you're on an expedition where you're having to find how far apart two people will be, if you have a communication thing and the communicating things will only travel so far... Examples would be, in baseball, you know how far away the batter is, so you know how far he can hit it. Or like in wars, where people calculate how far away you are from the army to set your guns and stuff like that.

Like Mike, Bram is able to see a mathematical relationship existing as a mental object *prior* to the writing of the word problem, a relationship *separable* from the concrete images of the word problem story. He is also willing and able to see such a mathematical relationship (referred to by "this" in his phrase, "I guess *this* could be practical") as projected onto other, perhaps more directly useful life situations. I think the development of this willingness to see mathematical relationships as having separability from and priority to life experiences and to see such relationships as objects possessing at least as much reality as those objects we can sense physically (touch, smell, taste, etc.) is one of the large goals of a mathematical education. In this sense, Bram and Mike have demonstrated a fairly direct reading of their teacher, Ibrahim's, intentions—that they be able to *see through* the stories of word problems to the mathematical structures underlying their composition.

The statistics students I interviewed also showed a high degree of thoughtfulness and accuracy in reading their teacher's intentions in assigning them word problems. Andrea, an engineering student who had worked in engineering firms for several co-op terms, saw the underlying mathematical structures of particular word problem types and saw a distinction between so-called "applied problems" and the actual work practices of engineers. She coined the interesting term "approaching reality" (perhaps parallel to the concept of a curve approaching an asymptote "in the limit"?) to describe the way word problems approximated life situations without actually touching them:

> Andrea: I remember doing the train problem with my dad one night. And then after that I could do the rest of them. Like this one reminded me, the car one, where he leaves at 50 miles and the other one's going at 35 miles per hour. That's a train problem. They're all basically the same.

> SG: Can you talk about that a little more? So now you can recognize train problems....

> Andrea: Yeah, just relate it. You can tell. It pretty much gives you the same kind of information in a different way. But basically, I don't know, it's like a structure, you can just put it into that again once you know how to do it the first time.

> SG: Is it a practical problem?

> Andrea: The train problem? I don't necessarily think they're always practical. I think they're modeled to approach practicality. Say something like a train problem—that's simplified. When I go on work terms—I'm in engineering—people don't actually tend to use math. They get a book that already did it for them, and then they look up the numbers. [laughs]

> They do approach practicality but I think that also they demonstrate that you have a good comprehension of what you've learned because you have to be able to apply it. It does approach practicality but not always. First of all they have to be cooked up to a certain degree to represent what you've just learned. If you're looking at them in a textbook, there'll be one topic that it will cover, or say one concept that you have to demonstrate knowledge of. So it's not really practical in that sense.

> SG: So it's always related to the topic of that chapter?

> Andrea: Well generally. That's been my experience specifically in dealing with textbooks. "We just taught you about this particular part of statistics and this formula so here's a word problem that is set up in such a way that you're going to use that."

Like Bram, Andrea has read her teacher's intentions fairly accurately. Robbins, her statistics teacher, commented earlier that "a word problem is a model of a real problem and then the mathematics is a model of the modelled problem. So there's a couple of steps of modeling. And how far from reality you get would vary from problem to problem." Andrea's assertions—that word problems "approach reality" but in a very simplified way and that word problem simplifications are tailored to reflect the focus topic of instruction—were very close to her teacher's earlier statements.

Andrea was also able to see particular word problem stories as exemplars of generic "types" like "the train problem." Again, like Bram and Mike, she saw a mathematical structure as separable from and prior to a particular word-problem story.

Both Andrea and her classmate Lisa saw in word problems the pedagogic intention of developing a habit of mind (recalling Bram's mention of a mathematical "mindset") and a generic problem-solving process. Interestingly, Andrea drew upon her engineering work experience to compare problem solving with design process:

> Lisa: If you do a lot of math word problems, sometimes when you look at some situation or something, it just goes quickly in your head that you analyze it according to math. Even a real-world problem … when you look at it you think, "OK, you have to do step one, step two, blah blah blah." You can apply it to anything. […] It trains you how to approach problems and solve problems. Sometimes I don't realize that I'm doing it but I look at problems and do problem solving according to math. After that—"What am I doing?" It's not math in here! [laughs] But still—I think it's just become a habit. Cause I really like math.

> Andrea: It's more, maybe, about learning the problem-solving process. Because that's sort of an interdisciplinary idea, something that you'll encounter in many areas of work that you're doing, is that you have a problem or a task. It's similar to, say, a design process. Actually, problem solving and design are similar in that you do this, for example, in engineering or in math. You have a design or a problem to confront, so you go through a set of steps. And word problems are one very good way to learn that process.

Sarah, another classmate, emphasized the "niceness" of the numbers used in most word problems as an example of the distance between "cooked-up" problems and those encountered in real life:

> Sarah: Real-life problems aren't in textbooks specifically, textbook problems are cooked up to be nice. Do a real problem and it's not nice.
>
> SG: Nice in terms of what?
>
> Sarah: They'll set up variables so that you have a nice answer. It will be four, or something and maybe you'll get terms that cancel and that's pretty and then you don't have to deal with a fifth-order differential problem.

In Ibrahim's earlier interview, he commented that one of his pedagogical intentions in using word problems was to provide familiar imagery for abstract mathematical concepts. Sarah, Andrea and their classmate Ken, who had tutored high school math students, commented in a similar way on this function of word problem imagery, which is close to the function of imagery in parables:

> Sarah : I was talking to my cousin the other day. There's a bus problem in here too, how you go out to catch a bus and it's different every day. [laughs] He was asking, "What's the difference between a discrete random variable and a continuous random variable?", and I used the bus example to tell him. So sometimes it's easier to relate, for someone who doesn't know, to be able to explain it using something that you can relate to.
>
> SG: A kind of example.
>
> Lisa: Yeah. Some kind of analogy. Using word problems—in a way, that helps.
>
> Andrea: Like teaching kids to add using apples …
>
> Ken: I've done tutoring for Grade 11 and Grade 12 math students, and I

would often have to reword the problem and then it would make sense. [...] I often found that if you just give them an equation in the middle of thin air, they'll probably be able to do it but they won't remember how to do it or why. But if you can somehow relate it to something useful—

SG: Can you give an example of one?

Ken: I was teaching my sister how to do polynomials and subdividing polynomials and splitting them up. I gave her some horrendous example about having to count Oreo cookies and how to count Oreo cookies on a curve and getting averages of Oreo cookies. She still remembers it and this was quite a while ago. So yes, it was a ridiculous example but she likes Oreo cookies and she ended up remembering it and now she remembers how to do that specific type of problem. She can just remember back to Oreo cookies. And also, I remember that a couple of weeks later she had another problem that she came and asked me about and I was able to say, "Well this is just like the Oreo cookie problem except you do this instead of this." And she said, " Oh. OK. Now I get it," and was able to move on from there. I guess that was one general example that I was able to use.

French Immersion Student Teachers

The student teachers in Krauss' mathematics education class were fluent bilingual French/English speakers who intended to teach in French-immersion elementary schools. Most of the student teachers in this group identified themselves as math phobic to some degree and as "language people" rather than "math people."

Their focus on the contingencies of language itself and their lack of familiarity with the linguistic tropes typical of word problems created difficulties for these students when working on mathematical word problems. For example, Krauss had recently given the class the following problem to work on:

Some children are seated at a *large* round table. They pass around a box of candy containing 25 pieces. Sue takes the first piece. Each child takes one piece of candy as the box is passed around. Sue also gets the last piece of candy, and she *could* have additional pieces. How many children could be seated around the table, including Sue? [italicized words my emphasis]

The student teachers fastened on the words "could," "large" and "some" and based their solution approaches to their interpretations of these words, none of which would have been considered standard mathematical interpretations:

> Sandy: And what do they mean by "could"? Could she if she wanted to? Could she if the other children didn't eat? ...

> Michel: When I read that I interpreted it, OK she gets the first and the last, so there's two less? So it can be anywhere from two children to 23 children? Because there's 25 pieces of candy. So two children to 23 children would give her the first and the last piece and would give her more if she wanted more....

> Anne: We all had different ways of doing it, so there was definitely room for interpretation there.

> Chris: Yeah, the "could have additional pieces" screwed everyone up because they weren't sure what that meant. Like "could have additional pieces" actually the last piece, or before the last piece, or....

> Sandy: ... In my mind "could have additional pieces" means, "if she feels like having the extra pieces that are left over, she can," so there's got to be at least one piece left and that's that. An option.

> Mark: ... It said "some children are seated at a LARGE round table. And I think in the answer, we could end up with a very small amount of children.... So anyway this thing gave me such a hard time that, if it had been written better, I would have spent more time actually doing the mathematical problem instead of trying to figure out the words that were.... When I saw "a large table" I thought, hey, there must be , like, twenty kids in there or something! I work by pictures. If I see "large round table" I see a lot of kids around a BIG table....

The curriculum writer's intended answer for the question, which Krauss later gave to the class, included several possible answers related to the factors of 24. The curriculum writer's "some" and "could" point to multiple possible answers that would satisfy the given situation. However, this group of student teachers, focusing on everyday language (rather than mathematical) uses of particular words and translations of quantifiers like "some" into specific number ranges, found the writer's given solution mystifying:

> Sandy: [reading the answer given to the problem]:"2, 3, 4, 6, 8, 12 or 24 children. Also one child if 'some' is not interpreted as more than one."

> Michel: "Some" starts at three. Two is "a couple." "Some" is three. Four is "a few."

> Anne: It's like "a few" and "a couple." "A few" is not two.... That's sort of a clue that you teach them when they are trying to start doing math problems. Start looking for things to know when to minus and add.

When I presented the word problem about the Tower of Pisa to this group, there was again a startlingly different interpretation of the wording itself, based on these students' focus on the contingencies of language rather than the purposes of mathematical pedagogy:

> A rock dropped from the top of the Leaning Tower of Pisa falls 6 metres from the base of the tower. If the height of the tower is 59 metres, at what angle does it lean from the vertical? (Ebos, Klassen & Zolis, 1990, p. 354)

> Stephanie: I could also see me thinking—cause I'm a tool—that the rock landed on some part of the tower that sticks out! So it landed six metres *above* the base.

The student teachers, in common with others working in elementary education, also tended to value real-life contingencies and problems more than abstract mathematical simplifications of problems. For example, I presented the group with the following word problem in French from an elementary school textbook:

> Cinq enfants pechent seize poissons. Ils se partagent les poissons également. Combien restera-t-il de poissons? [Five children catch sixteen fish. They share the fish equally. How many fish are left?]

Stephanie: If I didn't know about remainders though I'd be, like, "Why is there a fish left?"

Sandy: But that's probably what the lesson is, is it? Is it on remainders?

Michel: What was the problem we're solving? Of course the thing is knowing that people are greedy, they're for sure going to take three each, right? So there can be one left. Definitely. [...] There's no way I would think, OK, they were taking two each, and then there were six left at the end.

Secondary Students

Like the university math undergraduates and the student teachers, McKay's junior secondary students in Grades 8 and 9 noticed that the word problems in their textbook were unrealistic in terms of everyday reality:

Marie drove her eighteen-wheeler 1280 km from Calgary to Winnipeg in 15.2 hours. Part of the trip she drove in a snow storm at an average speed of 60 km per hour. The rest of the time she drove at 100 km per hour. How far did she drive in the storm? (Kelly, Alexander & Atkinson, 1987a, p. 205)

Sandra: She's driving 15 hours? Doesn't she stop for lunch or anything? Or to go to the washroom—

SG: Sleep, or—

Rick: Lunch, dinner and breakfast, fifteen hours—I could probably stay in the car for like, three hours at the most!

Sandra: I went 16 hours but we stopped. Not to sleep but just to eat and go to the bathroom.

Melodie: We drove from here to Disneyland. It took us about, I think, two days or something like that. But we still stopped and we slept in hotels and everything and had dinner. So we didn't—it was a long way but not like fifteen hours straight.

Rick: Non-stop. It's not really realistic, unless you fell asleep at the wheel.

Sandra: I don't think they're allowed to do that anyway. I think they're only allowed to do twelve hours or something, because of all those accidents that happen.

SG: I'm sure you're right.

Sandra: So I don't think that's very good.

Some of the students, particularly the younger students in Grade 8, treated word problems as enjoyable puzzles and found more pleasure in doing word problems than algorithmic math "number" questions:

Darrell: I've always like brain teaser kind of things. And just the challenge of doing them.... With sentence questions, it's more along the lines of a change of pace, something different. If you do twenty adding questions and then do a problem-solving question, it just changes, so it's more interesting.

SG: Why do you think these word problems are included in your textbook?

Penny: To make you really think about it and not just take out a calculator and, like, work the calculator. To make sure you really piece the puzzle together instead of just giving you a question... Or sometimes it will leave out one part and you have to figure that out before you can actually answer the question. So it actually makes you think more... For me, I'd rather have those kind of questions. For me it's a lot more fun than just a bunch of numbers or words.

SG: What makes it more fun?

Penny: Well, it's kind of like a puzzle. I like puzzles, like mysteries and stuff.

Darrell: It takes more thought to answer them.

Penny: And it makes you pay attention.

Even the Grade 9 students I interviewed, who generally dislike word problems, saw them as having some special value as puzzles and as sources of imagery, particularly if the problem involved topics they found attractive. From the first Grade 9 interview group:

SG: So why do they give you word problems in your math textbook?

Wanda: It makes you think differently. It makes you think in different terms than just giving you the numbers. You have to figure out the numbers sometimes.

Jennifer: It gives you an image of what you're learning.

Miriam: It can waste your time. [all laugh].

SG: Tell me about that.

Miriam: Or it makes you smart. [laughs]

SG: What do you mean by wasting your time?

Miriam: Sometimes if you don't have any—we have nothing to do. So we can do problem solving in order to waste the time.

SG: Like a hobby or something like that?

Miriam: Yeah.

Wanda: Kind of boring hobby though.

From the second Grade 9 interview group:

Rick: But there's different ones. There's, like, if a car, like, I don't know, goes back and forth from school five days a week and it uses this much gas—those ones are pretty real. And you have to figure out how much gas you use or whatever.

SG: So you guys aren't driving yet, are you? Cause you're not sixteen yet.

Rick: But soon!

For the most part, the Grade 9 students expressed negative emotional reactions to being assigned word problems for homework. From the first interview group:

SG: How do you feel when you're given these problems to do? What's your emotional reaction?

Darlene: Headache.

Miriam: Uncomfortable.

Jennifer: I'd moan.

SG: What is it about them that makes people moan and get a headache?

Jennifer: Too much thinking. I mean, you can't do ten things with your brain. One thing is enough. If you have a problem, you have two numbers, right? And you have a question with it too. You wouldn't understand all of it at once. So you have to sit there and think for half an hour and then you get the question right!

Miriam: When you take a hour to solve a problem and then you show it to your teacher and it's wrong, you might feel very sad.

Darlene: Yeah, sad. It's like you tried for so long but it's still wrong.

From the second interview group:

Melodie: I don't really understand any of them. I always have to read it over a lot because I'm not good with word problems.

SG: What makes them hard?

Sandra: They're so long.
Rick: There's so much information in one little story.

Sandra: Yeah. And most of it you don't even need.

Melodie: I think it's all the words too. I guess if you're used to just a question, like a multiplication question, you only multiply and it's already written out. But these ones, you have to figure out how to figure out the answer.

Rick: You have to figure out the question first and then you have to figure out the answer.

Sandra: Yeah! And there're so many filler words.

Melodie: Sometimes they add information that you don't need just to trick you, too.

SG: Why do they want to trick you?

Rick: Because they want to make you think.

Sandra: And to learn from your mistakes.

SG: Does it make you think, when you're tricked?

Rick: No, it just makes me go crazy. [All laugh] I want to throw my book out the window.

Elementary Students

When I interviewed Bertrand, the teacher of this Grade 5/6 elementary class, she expressed her own love of mathematical and other puzzles and her enjoyment in solving them. Her students seemed to have "read" fairly clearly her intentions with regard to the pleasure inherent in problem solving, intentions more closely allied to riddling traditions than to traditional mathematics education. These students expressed a sense of curiosity and eagerness about problem solving.

I wanted to find out whether the particular story in the word problem seemed to make a difference for the students. Their response was ambiguous. On one hand, they were able to "see through" the stories and abstract numbers and operations from word problems. At this level, they knew that the stories "didn't matter." On the other hand, they were attracted to problems that dealt with appealing subjects—like candy:

> 24. Mike had 52 tomatoes to put in bags of six. How many bags did he fill? How many tomatoes were left over?
> 25. Suzanne put 68 plums in cartons of 8. How many cartons did she fill? How many plums were left over?
> 26. Sandra put 47 apples in bags of 6. Adrian put 60 apples in bags of 8. Who had more apples left over? (Kelly et al., 1986, p. 129)

SG: Are these different problems or are these all the same problem?

Jessica: They're different. All different.

SG: Are they different because they're about Mike and Suzanne and Sandra? Tomatoes and plums?

Jessica: It doesn't matter about that. Tomatoes and plums and apples.... [That doesn't make a difference.] The numbers do.

SG: So if they said, "Mike had 52 bullets and he was putting them into a box," would that be the same question?

All three: Yeah.

SG: Would it bother you if it was about something like bullets? ...

Alex: It would be better if it was, like, rocket blasters.

Cathy: I'd, like, change it into another thing like candy or something.

Jessica: Just think of it differently if you don't like it that way.

Alex: Oh, I just had an idea. You know what I think. You'd have a better question, like if it's candy. Sometimes you think of that when you solve a problem. Then when you go home you want to have candy. So your mouth just makes you do the question.
Jessica: [moans] Oh, it's so good!
Alex: It sends a message to your brain.

Jessica: Sweet and crunchy!

Alex: You just do the question. And then you go home and have some. So it's like that.

These students saw the stories as adding interest to what would otherwise be a dry math problem, particularly because of the *question* component of the word-problem genre, which gave them a point of entry into the story:

> One Saturday the conservation club planted 387 coniferous trees. On Sunday they planted 593 trees. How many trees were planted in all? (Kelly et al., 1986, p. 29)
>
> SG: Why do they say "Saturday and Sunday"? Does it make any difference if it's Saturday and Sunday?... Does it make any difference if they say "coniferous trees"?
>
> All: No.
>
> SG: So when they were writing this question, why did they say "Saturday" and "Sunday" and "coniferous trees"?
>
> Charles: Because that was the day that popped into their mind....
>
> SG: So if they just said, "Three hundred and eighty-seven. Five hundred and ninety-three. How many altogether?" Would that still be the same question?
>
> Charles and Nancy: Yup.
>
> SG: Would it be an interesting question?
>
> Charles and Nancy: Nope.
>
> SG: Is it an interesting question with the trees?
>
> All: Yeah.
> SG: Why? What's the difference?

Nancy: Because you have a little story to read. And it kind of gives a little more excitement. Like when you're reading the question you're kind of excited to read what's going to happen next or what's the question and stuff like that.

SG: So what happens next in this story?

Nancy: You have to answer how many trees were planted.

SG: What if I told you a story and it wasn't in math class? If I said, "Alright, I'm going to tell you a nice story. Once upon a time I planted 593 trees. Then the next day I planted 387 trees. The end." Would that be a good story?

All: No. Yeah. No.

Lisa: Kind of dry.

Nancy: It's the same thing, but you're not actually asking us to answer it. But it is kind of interesting like that, but you didn't ask us to answer it. If you asked us to answer it it would be more interesting because we'd get to take part in it.

SG: Tell me more about that....

Nancy: If you said to me, "I planted 593 trees one day and I planted 397 the other day. How many trees do you think I planted?" then I would, like, have pleasure in answering that. But, like, if you just said that you planted this many and this many on this day, then you just ended it, then I'm like, "Fine, I heard it." But if you actually told me, "How much do you think?" then I have something to think about, something to get my brain working and stuff like that.

It was interesting to me to see that even if the story was dull in itself, it was still more interesting than a bare numerical algorithm problem which had no imagery attached to it. And the fact that all word problems offer a *point of entry*, a place to insert oneself actively into the story, was what gave pleasure and excitement to these students. Room for active involvement, a "living-space" for the reader within the story, however minimal a story it might be, seemed to make a difference on an imaginative level for these students and turned mere exercise into play.

Stories also seemed to matter if there were matters of real-life morality involved. When I used the "stutterers" word problem from my university statistics book as an example, the students fastened on the moral and ethical implications of the story:

> SG: What if a math problem had a story about something that really bothered you? There's one I had in one of my university textbooks about a psychological experiment. It said that they were treating people to see what would stop them from stuttering and they gave them electric shocks. So I started this problem and I said, "I don't want to do this problem because…"

> Jessica: That's an exciting one.

> SG: Well it seemed to me it was a kind of really cruel thing to do to somebody for stuttering. Every time they'd stutter, they'd give them an electric shot, like a jolt.

> Alex: Ugh.

> Jessica: Is that real?

> SG: Yeah, it really was real. It happened a long time ago, it was about thirty years ago… It was at the time when I was around Grade 5.

> Alex: If you stuttered in school when you were in Grade 5, would you get the shock too?

> SG: No, this was just something that was being done as an experiment. It wasn't done widely… So what if you were given a problem like this: "There were forty-five people who were in to get electric shock therapy for stuttering. They were arranged on nine benches. How many on each bench?"… Would it make the problem more interesting? Not so interesting? Would you want to do it? Would you not want to do it?

> Jessica: Exciting ones are easier to do…

> Cathy: You get more sense in you. I mean, they make more sense to you.

Alex: First I would think, why do you shock people? That's like, so bad. And then I would do the question. And then I'd have nightmares about that... Once I had a thing because a rabbit and I remember this dream that the rabbit killed me...

Jessica: If you're doing like a big presentation in front of lots of people, then maybe you'd stutter... Then they'd shock you... Did they kill them?

SG: No.

Alex: Did you *know* about that in Grade 5?

SG: No.

Alex: So you didn't know until, like, university.

SG: Yeah.

For these students, it seemed that a holistic, global view of the implications of the problem story took precedence over more abstract mathematization, particularly where the story was an engaging one with ties to real-life situations and to questions of morality and ethics. Although they were able to see that the story "didn't matter" if it seemed trivial or written specifically for a puzzle or math exercise, they were not willing to disengage their sense of what was right in the world if the word problem story dealt with real-life issues.

Conclusions

The students from elementary, secondary and tertiary levels of education interviewed took up the intentions embedded in word problems on several different levels simultaneously. Most of the students were able to "see through" word problem stories and abstract the mathematical structures the genre points to. At the same time, stories could matter and for various reasons. If the story was particularly absurd or troubling, it drew attention to itself and demanded some investment of energy before abstract mathematical structures could be attended to. For students focused on language, word choices and linguistic structures themselves could lend ambiguities unintended by teachers and curriculum writers to the word problems. The value of memorable imagery was noted by elementary and tertiary mathematics students, both as a mnemonic device and as an engaging element of story. Elementary students noted that a point of entry into the story (via the question component of the word problem) allowed for pleasure and involvement in solving the problem.

Generally speaking, the students all seemed to be good "readers" of their teachers' intentions and student interpretation of word problem intentions matched their teachers' stated intentions fairly closely. Students involved in levels of education closest to elementary school more often read word-problem intentions as embedded in everyday, real-life contexts, while those at the tertiary level in mathematics were more willing to move quickly to an abstraction of mathematical relationships without questioning the stories' real-life plausibility.

Chapter 7
The History of the
Word Problem Genre

I have added seven times the side of my square to eleven times its area and
it is 6;15.
—Babylonian problem BM 13901, 7, from Neugebauer, *Mathematische
Keilschrifttexte*, quoted in Aaboe, 1964, p. 23

You have 100 drachmas and you are told to buy 100 birds. Of the birds,
Ducks are sold at 2 drachmas each, Hens at 1 drachma, Doves at 2 for 1
drachma, Ringdoves at 3 for 1 drachma and Larks at 4 for 1 drachma.
How many of each type of bird was purchased?
—Abu Kamil, 900 A.D., in Olivastro, 1993, p. 188

A woman dies leaving a husband, a son and three daughters. She also
leaves a bequest consisting of $1/8 + 1/7$ of her estate to a stranger.
Calculate the shares of her estate that go to each of her beneficiaries.
—al-Khwarizmi's *Algebra*, in Joseph, 1992, p. 319

A certain man went to market three times. The first time he brought back
twice what he had taken with him. On the second trip he took with him
this double amount and returned with the same plus its square root plus
2 additional *aurei*. All this he preserved and he returned to market with
it a third time and his profit from this trip was the square of what he
took with him and 4 *aurei* in addition. He returned, moreover, with 310
aurei. I want to know, therefore, how much he took with him on his first
trip.
—Cardano, 1968: 1545, p. 44

A bamboo shoot 10 *ch'ih* tall has a break near the top. The configuration
of the main shoot and its broken portion forms a triangle. The top touches
the ground 3 *ch'ih* from the stem. What is the length of the stem left standing erect?
—*Chiu-chang suan-shu*, in Swetz & Kao, 1977, p. 44

If a hundredweight of cotton is worth 36 *ducats*, 10 *grossi*, 10 *pizzoli*,
what is the amount to be deducted for 8348 pounds, tare being 6 pounds

per hundred, and tret 2 *ducats* per hundredweight?

—Swetz, 1987, p. 134

Mathematical word problems have a very long history, perhaps as long as the history of human written records. A large proportion of the mathematical cuneiform writings discovered earlier in this century on 4,000-year-old clay tablets from ancient Babylon consist of solved word problems, as do the 3,500-year-old hieroglyphic writings on the Rhind papyrus from ancient Egypt. We have recorded examples of mathematical word problems from Ch'in Dynasty China (c. 300 B.C.), ancient and medieval India and medieval Europe and the Islamic world and a continuous record of word problems from early Renaissance Europe to present-day textbooks used in school mathematics around the world.

Some of the word problems still in circulation have been shown to be identical in their mathematical structures and often similar in their story "dressing" to problems that are thousands of years old. No one has set out deliberately to preserve these problems, yet while many other mathematical and literary forms have been lost or discarded over time, these word problems have persisted. Why?

Two related questions are addressed in this chapter. First, I ask whether the social and pedagogic purposes of word problems have remained stable over time. In this section, I find clues to the development of the word-problem genre in its historic links to oral traditions of riddles and contests, to practical calculation in "real-world" work situations and to the development of symbolic algebra.

Second, using the linguistic genre analysis developed in chapter 3, I ask whether the generic form of mathematical word problems has remained stable over their 4,000-year history. Since many of the oldest examples are written in languages unfamiliar to me (Ancient Akkadian and Ancient Egyptian, for example), I have consulted with experts in these fields in an effort to avoid problems of translation.

In reading historic texts that appear formally similar to problems in our own school textbooks, it is easy for us to read our own experiences of schooling onto past eras. Though this may have some benefit in providing us with empathy and insight into past times through connections to our own experience, it may also keep us from being able to imagine the "otherness" of previous eras and cultures. At the end of this chapter, I present a conjecture about differences in the purposes of word problems in different times.

Babylonian Word Problems: Were They Practical?

As a sixth-form student, I once got into an argument about applied mathematics at a university interview. Although I found the subject relatively easy, I did not like the way that problems were superficially about the "real world," but in fact were so contrived that they were meaningless. The interviewer, who of course turned out to be an applied mathematician, responded rather indignantly that if the problems were not contrived they would be impossibly difficult (for mere students) to solve. This was in the early nineteen-seventies, long before the notion of modeling became fashionable in school or university mathematics. Neither I nor the interviewer had any vocabulary available to bridge the gap between our differing perspectives. (Ainley, 1996, p. 1)

Hundreds of clay tablets containing "problem texts" from ancient Babylon have been found by archaeologists, most of them dating from the period 2000 to 1600 B.C. These problem texts are the second most frequently found text type on Babylonian tablets, after "table texts" containing multiplication, reciprocal, square root and other tables presumed to have been used as references by scribes. Another frequently found text type is the "teachers' list," which lists alternative number sets which give integral answers to particular problem types. These are hypothesized to have been used by teachers in composing new word problems in standard forms.

The problem texts include word problems, often many on the same topic, along with instructions for solution, the answer and/or a diagram. They are believed to be textbooks from

Babylonian scribal schools, which trained young people in literacy, bookkeeping and a variety of administrative duties. At first glance, the word problems appear to deal exclusively with practical problems of agricultural, commercial, legal and military administration—questions about grain stores, irrigation, inheritance, the construction of buildings and siege ramps. On account of the superficial "everyday" quality to the stories and the fact that the scribal schools were vocational training institutions, Babylonian mathematics has been characterized as "merely practical" as opposed to later Greek abstract, theoretical mathematics.

Some scholars who have looked more closely at the corpus of Babylonian word problem texts have come to different conclusions. The problem of deixis or reference in contemporary word problems appears to originate in the very earliest word problems, those from ancient Babylon. While some of the problems included in the problem texts could conceivably refer to practical situations encountered in the day-to-day working life of a Babylonian scribe, others are very far-fetched in terms of the numbers and dimensions used, the extreme simplification of a potential practical problem, or the nature of the unknown elements and the question posed. The impractical nature of these stories calls into question their referentiality in pointing to "real world" situations and casts doubt upon the serious practicality of even those more plausible problems.

Eleanor Robson, an Oxford Assyriologist with a mathematical background, writes:

> Should we think of [Babylonian mathematics] merely as a practical training for future overseers, accountants and surveyors? ... Take the topic of grain-piles as a starting point. In the first sixteen problems of BM 96954 [a Babylonian mathematical tablet in the British Museum] the measurements of the grain-pile remain the same, while each parameter is calculated in turn.... The first preserved problem concerns finding the volume of the top half of the pile. One could imagine how such techniques might be useful to a surveyor making the first estimate of the capacity of a grain-pile after harvest. However, then things start to get complicated.

The remaining problems give data such as the sum of the length and the top, or the difference between the length and the thickness, or even the statement that the width is equal to half of the length plus 1. It is hardly likely that an agricultural overseer would ever find himself needing to solve this sort of a problem in the course of a working day.

[In two other sets of problems] the pile is 10 nindan (60 m) long and 36–48 cubits (18–24 m) high. It is difficult to imagine how a grain pile this big could ever be constructed, let alone measured with a stick. (Eleanor Robson, personal e-mail communication, 21 January 1997)

Besides grain-piles as large as an eight-story office building and clearly impractical calculations involving unexpected combinations of their dimensions (recalling the "guess my age" word problems whose applicability continues to perplex many practical-minded students), Robson cites a Babylonian preference for integral measurements, even when it was clearly known that such measurements were inaccurate. For example, she refers to eight problems about right-angled triangles, which demonstrate three methods for finding the length of the diagonal of a 2- by 8-unit rectangle. Each of the three methods produces a different length for the diagonal. When the length of the diagonal is given at the start of the problem (and the solver is to find the length of one of the other two sides), it is not the most accurate measurement which is given but the one which produces an integer answer with the method of solution used.

Robson argues that it is inappropriate to draw a dichotomy between "pure" and "applied" or "practical" Old Babylonian mathematics since the problems functioned on two levels. On one hand, they taught practical skills and tested methods to future scribes; on the other hand, "many of those methods no longer had real-life applications," and the problems extended once-practical skills to story situations that were clearly not referring to everyday life.

Robson's concept of a Babylonian mathematics which was at once potentially useful and obviously impractical is appealing and

can be used to analyze contemporary mathematics. Her deliberately ambiguous view of ancient mathematics offers a way out of
our current dualistic "pure/applied" categories which seem unsat-
isfactory ways to describe the work of most mathematicians. In
looking at the history of word problems, it is also interesting that
the question, "Are they real-life problems?" can be extended back
to the earliest examples of the genre and that ambiguous answers
to that question can be traced in a continuous line back to the origins of written mathematics.

Jens Høyrup, a Danish Assyriologist and historian of mathematics, refers to a Babylonian problem about the construction of a
siege ramp in his argument about the non-applied nature of some
Babylonian problems. Although the problem appears on the surface to have a practical military application, Høyrup notes that
the problem solver is supposed to be able to know the "amount of
earth required for its construction together with the length and
height of the portion already built but not the total length and
height to be attained." He comments that

> many [second-degree problems in Babylonian problem texts] look like
> real-world problems at first; but as soon as you analyze the structure of
> known versus unknown quantities, the complete artificiality of the prob-
> lems is revealed.... As scribal discourse in general, mathematical dis-
> course has been disconnected from immediate practice; it has achieved a
> certain autonomy. (Høyrup, 1994, p. 7)

Høyrup characterizes Old Babylonian mathematics as based
on *methods* where Greek mathematics grew out of *problems*—and
this despite the fact that nearly all the Babylonian texts we have
are problem texts, which delineate methods only through repeated
solved examples. Høyrup's distinction is between Babylonian
scribal school mathematics, which aimed to train students in
methods available at hand rather than in an understanding of
these methods and Greek mathematics, which aimed to solve
problems (like doubling the cube, trisecting the angle and squaring
the circle) by extending mathematics and devising new methods.

He comments that many of the "useless second-degree problems" included in the Babylonian texts "appear to have been chosen not because of any inherent interest but just because they *could be solved* by the methods at hand." (Høyrup, 1994, p. 7)

This analysis appears to use an anachronistic application of contemporary valuations of "training" and "education" (i.e., skills training as inferior to educated understanding). But I think that Høyrup's point is a more subtle distinction in terms of discourses available to the Babylonians and the Greeks. It is important to remember that Babylonian documents predate Greek ones by some 1500 years and that the Babylonians may have been the first people in the world to conceive of mathematics as a unified and distinct area of study. Høyrup writes,

> There were no social sources, and no earlier traditions, from which a concept of mathematics as an activity per se could spring, and there was thus no possibility that a scribe could come to think of himself as *a virtuoso mathematician*. Only the option to become a *virtuoso calculator* was open; so, Babylonian "pure mathematics" was in fact calculation pursued as *art pour l'art*, mathematics applied in its form but disengaged from real application. (Høyrup, 1994, p. 8)

He does not imply that the Babylonians were incapable of "pure mathematics" but that they had no other discourse available other than that of practical problems to express abstract mathematical ideas. Høyrup writes, "Even when Old Babylonian mathematics is 'pure' *in substance*, it remains *applied in form*. In contradistinction to this, the prototype of Greek mathematics is pure in form as well as in substance" (p. 8).

On the other hand, Jacob Klein, writing about Diophantus, reserves the notion of "purity of form" for modern symbolic algebra. For him, Diophantus' mathematics was an intermediate stage bridging the "rhetorical algebra" of problems stated in words and ordinary language, and the abstract symbolic algebra of modern mathematics:

> We must not forget that *all* the signs which Diophantus uses are merely
> word abbreviations.... For this reason Nesselmann (*Algebra der
> Griechen*, p. 302) called the procedure practiced by Diophantus a "syn-
> copated algebra" which, he said, forms the transition from the early
> "rhetorical" to the modern "symbolic" algebra (according to Nesselmann
> even Vieta's mode of calculation belongs to the stage of syncopated alge-
> bra). (Klein, 1968, p. 146)

Again the questions raised in discussion of Babylonian word
problems can be viewed in a way that reflects on our use of word
problems in contemporary school mathematics. Are word problems used primarily to train students in the use of methods without necessarily providing an understanding of those methods? Are
problems chosen simply to illustrate the "methods at hand"?
(Certainly the evidence from curriculum writers like Lidstone in
Chapter 5 seems to indicate at least a projection of known methods onto the experienced world to create word problems with
"nice numbers" and available methods of solution.)

Similarly, we could ask whether our need for the concrete imagery of word problems has changed, since we have access to
post-Greek abstract mathematical discourse and symbolic algebra.
I will discuss this question further toward the end of this chapter.

The History of Word Problems and Riddles, Puzzles and Recreational Mathematics

I have argued that mathematical word problems are generically
non-referential and that it is inappropriate to assign truth value to
them—they flout the Gricean maxim of quality. That is to say,
even when word-problem stories appear to refer to aspects of the
"real world," their links to the world of lived experience are ambiguous at best. So why are these rather fanciful stories included
at all?

I raised this question in correspondence with mathematician
David Singmaster of South Bank University, London. Singmaster,
who has done extensive research into the history of recreational
mathematics, replied:

Many problems in recreational mathematics are embellished with a story which is often highly improbable, and this is partly what makes the problem memorable and recreational. However, I don't know which came first, the problem or the story. In many cases, the story is essential to make the problem interesting. For example, I once saw an exam schedule where six two-and-a-half hour exams was typed as 62 1/2 hour exams. The first takes 15 hours and the second takes 31 hours. When can they be equal? This formulation is much more interesting than, "Find numbers a, b, c, d such that a * (b + c/d) = ab * c/d." (David Singmaster, personal e-mail communication, 12 December 1996)

Singmaster's comments raised several issues, including the question of the sheer pleasure of story and particularly nonsensical story, in word problems and the historic and generic relationship between word problems in schools and orally transmitted riddles in social settings.

Høyrup has addressed both these questions to some degree in his writing on Babylonian word problems. He quotes Hermelink (1978, p. 44) who describes recreational mathematics as "problems and riddles which use the language of everyday but do not much care for the circumstances of reality." "'Lack of care' is an understatement," writes Høyrup and echoes Singmaster in saying that:

a funny, striking, or even absurd deviation from the circumstances of reality is *an essential feature* of any recreational problem. It is this deviation from the habitual that causes amazement, and which thus imparts upon the problem its recreational value. (Høyrup, 1994, pp. 27- 29)

Using "the language of everyday" but "not much caring for the circumstances of reality" is also a very apt characterization of the non-referential nature of both word problems and parables as genres. As shown above, a "lack of care for the circumstances of reality" has been a feature of word problems as early as the Old Babylonian period. Høyrup posits a continuum of non-referential story problems ranging from the most delightful mathematical recreations to the dullest of school exercises:

One function of recreational mathematics is that of teaching.... This end of the spectrum of recreational mathematics passes imperceptibly into general school mathematics, which in the Bronze Age as now would often be unrealistic in the precision and magnitude of numbers without being funny in any way. Whether funny or not, such problems would be determined *from the methods to be trained*.... Over the whole range from school mathematics to mathematical riddles, the methods or techniques are thus the basic determinants of development, and problems are constructed that permit one to bring the methods at hand into play. (Høyrup, 1994, pp. 27–29)

Work by the German mathematics historian Tropfke (1980), Singmaster (1988) and others has established the often-ancient provenance and wide historical, geographic and cultural distribution of a large number of famous word-problem/recreational-problem types. For example, the "cistern problem" referred to in Chapter 3, the "purchasing a horse" problem, the "100 birds" problem and the "crossing a river" problem have appeared in ancient India and China, medieval Byzantium and the Islamic world and in medieval and Renaissance Europe. The familiar children's riddle in English, "As I was going to St. Ives", has been traced back to a problem in the Rhind papyrus and is related to a problem from Sun Tzu in ancient China, and the famous Islamic-Indian "chessboard problem" can be traced to Babylonian origins, as well as related problems in China and in Europe (in Alcuin, for example). As Høyrup points out, "the same stock [of widely known story problems] was also drawn upon by Diophantus, who, of course, stripped the problems of their concrete dressing." (Høyrup, 1994, p. 35)

Høyrup relates the very wide distribution and longevity of these famous problems to an oral tradition of recreational problem riddles transmitted by merchants along the Silk Route:

Like other riddles, recreational mathematics belongs to the domain of oral literature. Recreational problems can thus be compared to folktales. The distribution of the "Silk Route group" of problems is also fairly similar to the distribution of the "Eurasian folktale", which extends "from Ireland to India."... However, for several reasons (not least because the outer limits of the geographical range do not coincide) we should not make too much of this parallel. Recreational problems belong to a specific subculture—the subculture of those people who are able to grasp them. The most mobile members of this group were, of course, the merchants, who moved relatively freely or had contacts even where communication was otherwise scarce (mathematical problems appear to have diffused into China well before Buddhism). (Høyrup, 1994, pp. 34–35)

The notion that recreational mathematics problems were orally transmitted across Europe and Asia is supported by observations from other writers on the history of mathematics. Dominic Olivastro cites the following examples of problems from Alcuin:

A certain gentleman ordered that ninety measures of grain were to be moved from one of his houses to another, thirty half-leagues away. One camel was to transport the grain in three journeys, carrying thirty measures on each journey. A camel eats one measure each half-league. How many measures will be left, when all has been transported?
(Alcuin of York, in Olivastro, 1993, p. 131)

A merchant in the East wanted to buy a hundred animals for a hundred shillings. He ordered his servant to pay five shillings for a camel, one shilling for an ass, and to buy twenty sheep for a shilling. How many camels, asses, and sheep were involved in the deal?
(Alcuin in Olivastro, 1993, p. 133)

and comments:

Camels appear often enough in these puzzles to raise a few suspicions... Why would an English monk [Alcuin] frame his puzzles in terms of an animal he probably never saw? The answer is that the puzzle, like many in the *Propositiones*, originated in the Middle East. The Arabs had already learned of the positional number system from the Indians, who in turn may have received it from the Chinese. The puzzles are from a very talented people; the solutions [that Alcuin gives] are not...[Alcuin] gives the wrong answers, or misunderstands the problems, or fails to find the general principle behind them. (Olivastro, 1993, p. 133)

Olivastro also quotes the following variants on the "crossing the river" problem from Alcuin:

> Three men, each with a sister, needed to cross a river. Each one of them coveted the sister of another. At the river, they found only a small boat, in which only two of them could cross at a time. How did they cross the river, without any of the women being defiled by the men? (Alcuin, *Propositiones*, problem 17, in Olivastro, 1993, p. 136)

> [A range of patriarchal assumptions underlie this word problem's story. Readers interested in questions of political values embedded in word problem stories are referred to Maxwell (1988).]

> A man had to take a wolf, a goat, and a cabbage across the river. The only boat he could find could take only two of them at a time. But he had been ordered to transfer all of these to the other side in good condition. How could this be done?
> (Alcuin, *Propositiones*, problem 18, in Olivastro, 1993, p. 138)

… and reports the following unattributed anthropological lore:

> In the Swahili tradition, a visitor from another region visits a sultan but refuses to pay tribute. He is confronted with a challenge: He must carry a leopard, a goat, and some tree leaves to the sultan's son who lives across a river, and he must use a boat that will hold only the visitor and two other items. The problem, of course, is that no two items can be left on the shore together….The visitor, after mulling over the problem, decides to carry first the leaves and goat, return with the goat, and then carry the goat and the leopard together to the son.

> A similar idea is found in Zambia. This time there are four items to transport: a leopard, a goat, a rat and a basket of corn, where each is likely to eat the one following it. The boat can hold only the man and one item. The story tells us that the man considers leaving behind the rat or the leopard and thus reducing the problem to the one of the Swahili tradition, but, the story goes, the man finally realizes that all animals are his brothers—so he decides not to make the trip at all! (Olivastro, 1993, p. 139)

I would have viewed these "exotic tales" as suspiciously pat had it not been for a similar report, this time from the Atlas mountains of Morocco, from a scrupulously reliable source, Eric Muller of Brock University (Muller, 1994). Muller's account is notable as it is the only first hand report of such practices that I have been able to find.

Muller visited several remote villages in the Atlas mountains on a number of occasions, accompanied by a Moroccan colleague, Professor Ha Oudadess of Rabat. In 1979, Oudadess had carried out a survey of oral mathematics traditions in the Atlas and was able to translate conversations from Berber into French for Muller.

Here is Muller's account of his experience of a living oral tradition of mathematical problem solving:

> It was in [the isolated village of] Tizin'Isli, on the terrace of the only cafe in town, over the inevitable cup of sweet mint tea, that we talked to Qlla Ikhlef. He speaks only Berber, which [Professor] Ha [Oudadess] translates for me into French.... He was born in 1962, in a small village higher up in the mountains.... He has no formal education but recalls that at the age of fourteen he was allowed to sit with some elders who would spend time inventing and solving problems. Can he recall any of the problems? "Oh yes."

> "Three people own 30 she-goats. In the spring 10 of them bear 3 kids, 10 bear 2 kids and 10 bear 1 kid. The three owners decide to split the herd equally so that they have the same number of goats and kids. No kid is to be separated from its mother. How can we do this?" ...

> Qlla recalls a social "problem competition" between men from his village and others from a different village. This would be held at the time of the souk (the travelling market which, in small villages, is held once a week.) On warm nights, before the souk, men would gather in an open tent, drink sweet mint tea, talk and sometimes pose problems for members from the other village to answer. We wonder where this tradition comes from. What in this culture makes mathematics problem solving a social activity? We know it is quite old because Ha remembers that as a youngster, in the Atlas, he was stopped and challenged by elderly men from the village to solve problems. It is also quite extensively spread throughout the Moroccan Atlas...

> The word has spread that these strangers, in shorts, are interested in

problems. A group of men come forward, one of them wants to share a problem. It is a version of the river-crossing involving a boat, a wolf, a goat and a cabbage, reworded for the local situation. No one else in the crowd has a problem to share...

Here are a couple more problems gathered by Ha [elsewhere in the Atlas].

1) A person wishes to purchase 100 birds using exactly 20 rials. For one rial the person can get either one hawk, or two pigeons or five sparrows. The person must buy at least one bird of each type. How many of each type can the person buy?

2) Three people go to the barber. To pay each person opens a drawer and places a payment equal to what is found in it and then closes the drawer. After the customers have left the barber finds 10 rials in the drawer. He wants to know how much each person paid. (Muller, 1994)

In the course of interviewing mathematics teachers for this book, I heard another anecdote about word problems, which in some ways was similar to Muller's (for example, in its portrayal of word problems embedded in a riddling tradition and as part of traditional village life). "Mohammed Ibrahim," a Canadian university mathematics professor who grew up in Iran, told me this story about an experience he had as a child.

When I was in Grade 10 I had a bike and used to ride it to the high school. I had a friend with no bike. So we had to double-ride but that was illegal in Iran. One day we were stopped by the police. My friend said something insulting to the police officer, so he had to take us to the station.

At the station there was a higher-ranking officer who was a nice guy. First, he asked us, "Why did you do this? Why did you insult the police officer?" Then he asked us what we were studying and we said mathematics. So he said, "You're students of math. Solve this one problem and I'll let you go. Otherwise I'll have to call your parents."

Here is the problem he gave us. Suppose you have a grocery shop and you're selling flour by the ounce, in amounts from one ounce to forty ounces. Can you find only four weights with which you could weigh out all whole-number amounts of flour, from one to forty ounces?

We struggled for an hour at the police station, but we couldn't solve the problem. However, luckily for us, the officer was a very nice man. He said, "You students these days don't know anything! I'll let you go—but I want you to solve this problem and come back to tell me the answer." So he let us go and we went on to school.

When I went to bed that night I thought and thought about this problem. It was a kind of obsession. And I can say that I solved it in my sleep! When I woke up in the morning, I knew the answer without knowing why it was true. You could measure all the possible amounts from one to forty ounces with four weights of 1, 3, 9 and 27 ounces. I'm not sure if I worked it out by process of elimination or what but I knew that it would work.

So I did go back to the police officer and told him the solution. He asked me how I got the answer. I asked him where he got the question. He said he was visiting a small village where there was this man who was selling things by the ounce but the man had only four weights for his scale. The officer asked the man, "Can you do all the weights with just that?" "Yes," said the man, "at least, I can do all the weights from one to forty!"

Years later, I came across the same problem, stated with more generality, in a book on number theory.

A Summary and a Conjecture

Looking closely at examples from the history of word problems in mathematics education, it seems evident that these problems were never intended solely for the purpose of applying mathematics to the solution of real-life problems. From the earliest of recorded word problems in Babylonian texts, word problems used unrealistic numbers, impractical situations and questions that would never arise in real-life problem situations. Although word problems superficially appeared to refer to real-life situations, their purpose was clearly not simply to solve actual difficulties encountered in day-to-day life.

Rather, they seem to have offered a way of exemplifying or embodying mathematical concepts and methods. We can imagine a teacher in an earlier era with an elegant mathematical method at hand, searching for ways of fleshing out or dressing up that method in terms of a story that drew on real-life references.

Certainly my research with contemporary Canadian curriculum writers and teachers shows this mode of writing word problems exists in our own times. A writer of calculus materials begins to look at the world with "calculus eyes," looking for examples of, say maxima and minima or rates of change in the world around, examples which can be simplified and given "nice numbers" to create word problems for students. A writer of primary school textbooks similarly sees the world with "addition and subtraction" and "regrouping" eyes, noticing things that increase and diminish, things that come grouped in packages of ten and so on. So, selectively viewing the everyday world, the calculus teacher may notice the acceleration patterns in the launching of a model rocket in the park, or the different rates the minute and second hands sweep out on the face of a clock; the elementary teacher may notice how many candies come in a roll or how many party hats are in a package; the intermediate teacher, teaching fractions and multiplication, may focus on cutting pizzas or doubling recipes. All may feel that the world is chock-a-block with examples of "their" mathematics. Of course, this may not seem so evident to others, including their own students. (Other disciplines impose their own special ways of making sense of everyday phenomena, too—a painter, a poet or a politician might feel that all the world's a play of colors, of words or of power struggles.)

The impulse for writing word problems begins with the structures and methods of mathematics and looks for ways of clothing these in stories from our lived lives. So the words in word problems do not actually refer to "real-life" objects and happenings in their full range of meanings and properties but only to those abstracted qualities which are isomorphic to the particular mathematical structure being illustrated. Most of our practical knowledge of the everyday world must be left behind when dealing with the stories of word problems. In these stories, there is no friction, no spillage, no unevenness or lack of uniformity—the contingencies of the world we know are deliberately omitted and any student who knows too much about the purported real-life subject of a word problem is well advised to leave that knowledge aside during math class. Word problems are not *about* the world we live in; they are about the world of mathematics.

And yet, in recent years, there has been a great deal of emphasis on giving students more and better word problems so that students will become "better problem-solvers" in the real-life world of work. In fact, since the Renaissance, mathematics textbooks have emphasized work-related word problems in terms of their practicality and applicability to real-life problem solving situations. Why?

My conjectured answer to this question is as follows: Before algebra, there was no means of stating mathematical generalities except by the use of examples. For example, the Babylonians had no general way of stating quadratic equations but repeated examples of word problems involving the area of square such as the following solved problem give a general method for solving quadratic equations:

> I have added the area and two thirds of the side of my square and it is 0;35. You take 1, the "co-efficient." Two thirds of 1, the coefficient, is 0;40. Half of this, 0;20, you multiply by 0;20 (and the result) 0;6,40 you add to 0;35 and the result 0;41,40 has 0;50 as its square root. 0;20, which you multiplied by itself, you subtract from 0;50 and 0;30 is the (side of) the square. (Babylonian problem quoted in Aaboe, 1964, p. 23)

Carrying out the solution procedure detailed in this and numbers of similar problems in the Babylonian texts yields a method for finding roots of a quadratic.

Is this question really about the area of a square? Aaboe notes that this and other similar problems are anything but practical problems. Aaboe writes:

That we are asked to add areas and lengths shows clearly that no real
geometrical situation is envisaged. In fact, the term "square" has no more
geometrical connotation than it does in our algebra. (Aaboe, 1964, p. 25)

Aaboe remarks that, although the Babylonians had no general
formula for the quadratic formula, working through the large number of solved word problems given in the Babylonian corpus
would ensure that one was familiar with a general procedure that
gives roots of quadratics.

In a similar way, Aaboe (p. 44) notes that what we now call
the "geometric algebra" of the ancient Greeks gives proofs we
would now consider to be fundamentally algebraic in terms of geometric imagery. He gives the example of Book II of Euclid's
Elements, which he says consists of theorems "which on the
surface belong to geometry, but whose contents are entirely
algebraic" (Aaboe, 1964, p. 44). Like the Babylonians, the Greeks
had no symbolism for expressing "ab" or "x^2" in the ways familiar
to us today, but those concepts could be expressed through
geometric images like "the area of a rectangle with sides of length
[a] and [b]", or "the area of a square with a side [x] units long."

My conjecture about the changing pedagogic purposes is
closely related to changes that came with the introduction of algebra from the Islamic world into the European world in the early
Renaissance. If word problems were used as a way of expressing
generality through repeated examples in pre-algebraic times, what
was their purpose once algebra provided a much more compact
way of stating general mathematical situations?

Word problems in Renaissance arithmetic books were largely
concerned with commercial dealings and many of these books
were written for an audience from the rising merchant class, who
studied arithmetic (or sent their sons to study from an arithmetic
master) for ostensible use in trade. These word problems retained
the formal structure of earlier word problems, which have had a
continuous history from Babylonian times and continue to be written in much the same standardized form. What may have changed

at the time of the introduction of algebra is the stated pedagogic purpose, or *pretext*, for including word problems as part of the mathematics teaching curriculum. Where in earlier times, the superficially practical story was inseparable from the underlying generality expressed through numerous repetitions of similar problems, algebra allowed a separation of these two functions. Because word problems were cut loose from their necessary role in stating mathematical generality, their use had to be shored up by a sometimes spurious emphasis on their practicality and applicability. Since Renaissance times at least and certainly in our own day, we have seen many instances of the use of word problems being justified by their practicality and usefulness, although studies like Lave (1992) and Nunes, Schliemann & Carraher (1993) have done much to prove that practical, applied mathematics in work situations are often quite different from the word-problem forms and solution methods taught in schools.

It is also interesting to note that, since students are rarely introduced to algebra before the age of fourteen or fifteen years, students themselves are "pre-algebraic" for most of their school mathematics career. Even when algebra has been introduced, most school students are not yet sufficiently familiar and fluent with algebra to accept algebraically stated generalities. So the use of word problems in contemporary schooling may be parallel in some ways to their use in pre-algebraic times, since they may be offered as repeated exemplars offering generality to students who are pre-algebraic or novices at algebra.

If my conjecture holds true—that is, if the format of word problems has survived and thrived for 4,000 years while its purposes have changed from riddles to exemplars of mathematical generality to practical, applied problems—then this might offer some encouragement to those of us who want to improve mathematics education through innovation in pedagogic practices. Without discarding word problems, which I believe have a great deal of cultural and historical interest, perhaps we can use them with new purposes. For example, we could find new ways of teaching with word problems through analogy with closely-related generic forms like riddles, koans and parables; rather than treating problems as disposable items, we could take time with each one, exploring its paradoxes, ambiguities and connections and allowing it to resonate with our lives as we would with a parable. Since word problems are never quite "about" the objects, people and places they purport to refer to, it might be useful to work with students on recognizing superficially different story problems with similar underlying mathematical structures. And word problems, with their long history, provide a natural link to the study of the history of mathematics.

Rather than treating word problems in either a staunchly traditionalist mode or sweeping them out of the mathematics curriculum in a bid for radical educational reform, I would prefer to resee them against different contextual backgrounds and reuse them in new ways and for new purposes. For those who value tradition, there may be consolation in knowing that this seems to have been an accepted practice throughout the history of mathematics education.

Chapter 8
Conclusions: What Does This Mean for Us As Teachers?

In the first chapter of this book, I raised several important questions about word problems as a genre in mathematics education and suggested that "taking a walk" around the genre, seeing it as an object from different points of view, could open up an understanding of the genre and how it could be used in teaching. In this final chapter, I will revisit my original questions in light of the findings detailed in Chapters 2 to 7 and make some suggestions about ways to improve teaching practice using insights gained from this analysis.

A Summary of Earlier Chapters

In chapter 2, I offered some background to genre theory from linguistics, literary studies and film studies, including the following assertions:

- Genres are sets of cultural conventions. Genres are defined by cultural recognition and consensus and do not necessarily satisfy a defining list of clearly stated characteristics.
- Addressivity is an important feature to investigate in any genre. A particular genre addresses a particular imagined audience.
- Examples of a certain genre are made in imitation, not of life but of other exemplars of the genre. (So word problems are made not in imitation of life but of other word problems.)
- To quote rhetorician Carolyn Miller, "What we learn when we learn a genre is not just a pattern of forms or even a method of achieving our own ends. We learn, more importantly, what ends we may have." (Miller, 1984, p. 165) The genres of our culture define us, our identities and desires, in

relation to our culturally mediated worlds.

• Genres carry their own generic intentions, which may or may not be our intentions as users of the genre. These meanings, inherent in the very form of the genre, may have historical or archaic roots.

In chapter 3, I looked at word problems from the point of view of linguistics and of literary theory. I asked two questions: what *is* the word-problem genre and what other genres is it *like*?

Linguistic analysis of the word-problem genre found the following features typical of word problems as a genre:

• A three-component narrative structure (set up, data, question).
• Indeterminate deixis of nouns and pronouns.
• A non-deictic use of metalinguistic verb tense.
• Strong, unambiguous illocutionary force (along the lines of, "Turn this into a mathematical problem of the type you have just been taught and find the right answer!"). This illocutionary force rests on a series of tacit assumptions—for example, that the word problem contains sufficient information for its solution, that contingencies of our lived lives cannot be invoked nor extraneous information requested, that the word problem can be turned into a symbolic mathematical problem, that a right answer exists, that word problems are meant as exercises to practice mathematical methods, etc.
• "No truth value"—that is, as with fiction, it is inappropriate to ascribe truth or falsity to the statements in a word problem.
• A flouting of the "Gricean maxim of quality" (which states that, in order to make conversation possible, we agree not to say what we believe to be false).

Literary analysis of word problems suggests that they are *like* religious or philosophical parables in their non-deictic, "glancing" referential relationship to our experienced lives and in the fact that the concrete images they invoke are interchangeable with other images without changing the essential nature of the word problem or parable. The nouns and verbs in both word problems and parables point to a non-material world (the world of mathematical objects or philosophical entities) rather than to their usual referents in our material, lived lives. For this reason, both parables and mathematical word problems feature odd, often fanciful, elliptical and inconclusive story elements, an anomalous use of verb tense and a lack of concern with the contingencies of day-to-day life.

Where the two genres differ is in their use. While parables are meant to be lingered over, because they resonate with the deepest concerns of human life and teach through paradox and perplexity, mathematical word problems are typically offered to students for quick translation into symbolic form, correct solution by familiar methods as an exercise, and immediate disposal.

Chapters 4, 5 and 6 looked at the word-problem genre as an object of pedagogy and looked at gaps between pedagogic intentions consciously ascribed to by teachers and writers, those inherent in the genre and those taken up by students in their role as cultural interpreters. In interviews with teachers and curriculum writers, a variety of stated pedagogic intentions were found. A pattern that emerged was that educators involved in elementary schooling valued practical, contextualized, open-ended problems over abstractly mathematical ones, while those in tertiary education valued abstract mathematical interpretations, in which students were encouraged to "see through" the apparent story to a mathematical structure (or alternately, to "project" the desired mathematics onto the story situation) rather than dwell on the given story. The only secondary teacher interviewed seemed to be in an uncomfortable middle position, pulled by the expressed aims of both elementary and tertiary mathematics education cultures. This teacher expressed conflicting desires to do "real" problem solving of the type favored by the elementary teachers and to acculturate students to see the abstract mathematical structures favored by tertiary education teachers.

Students' interpretations of their teachers' intentions seemed quite accurate—that is to say, the students were skilled readers of their teachers. Those with the highest levels of tertiary mathematics education were most consistently willing and able to "see through" word problems to mathematical structures and, although some initially stated that word problems were meant to prepare them for practical job situations, a look at some examples from their own textbook led them to other conclusions.

Elementary and junior secondary students, although capable of "seeing through" story as well, more often looked at word problems in terms of their real-life applications, in terms of their holistic meanings and lived-life contingencies. They criticized particular problems on practical or moral grounds. Those students whose teacher enjoyed the pleasurable riddling tradition affiliated historically with word problems also expressed enjoyment at solving puzzles. Students valued the interest and memorability of word problem imagery and saw the question component as a point of entry to become involved in playing with the problem.

In Chapter 7, I looked at the history of the word-problem genre, focusing on issues of intentionality. It was found that mathematical word problems have a continuous history going back more than 4000 years, to ancient Babylon and ancient Egypt and spanning cultures as diverse as ancient China, medieval India, the medieval Islamic world and medieval and Renaissance Europe. What is more, the form of mathematical word problems appears nearly unchanged throughout its long history.

It was established that, from the earliest citations of word problems on Babylonian clay tablets, these problems were never simply applications of mathematics to practical, real-life problems. Mathematical methods and concepts have always come prior to the stories of word problems and there has always been ambiguity in the referents for the words in these stories. In a tangential way, the words used refer to the concrete objects that are their usual referents in natural language; however, their primary referents are the objects and methods of a mathematical world although these are only spoken of in the coded clothing of story.

I speculated that the purpose of mathematical word problems may have changed at the time when algebra was introduced. In a pre-algebraic culture, the only way to express mathematical generality may be through repeated exemplars—that is, through a series of stories which point to similar mathematical structures and methods. Algebra, on the other hand, can easily express generality using variables. My conjecture is that, once algebra had been introduced, the long tradition of word problems was preserved by attaching new meaning to the genre, that of useful, practical problems. The pretext of practicality and usefulness has justified the use of word problems in mathematics education, and since most school students are either pre-algebraic or novices at algebra, word problems may continue to serve the purpose of expressing generality through repeated exemplification for them.

Some Implications for Teaching

Is there a distinction between riddles, recreational puzzles and school word problems? Since the same problems can be found contextualized in all three settings, the difference seems to lie mainly in the intentions surrounding the problem. Riddles are contextualized in a setting of pleasurable social interaction. They can be part of a process of building social solidarity and, simultaneously, a source of competition as in the village riddling contests. Although riddles have been collected in written form, their primary use is in oral culture and good riddlers can draw from a large memorized repertoire upon which a certain degree of improvisation is possible.

In contrast, word problems in school mathematics are traditionally assigned as a sort of bitter medicine that will make you better. In North American mathematics textbooks, they usually come at the end of a series of "easier" numerically or algebraically stated problems related to a mathematical concept introduced in the preceding chapter. The word problems represent a final test of students' competence in recognizing problem types related to that chapter and translating those problems into tractable diagrams and equations which can be solved using taught algorithmic methods. School word problems are not social events nor part of an oral culture. They are ideally meant to be solved silently, individually, using pencil and paper. Students are certainly not encouraged to memorize a repertoire of word problems for later enjoyment. On the contrary, once solved, they are generally discarded by teacher and students.

Riddles often retain strong links to folktales and parables and other teaching tales in their invocation of paradox and ambiguity, through their use of puns, hyperbole, nonsense, etc. Like parables and word problems, they point to two worlds at once—the world of their literal referents and another world invoked by word play or unexpected associations and structures. In riddles and parables, this ambiguity is embraced as essential to the enjoyment and philosophical import of the genre.

Contemporary writers of mathematical word problems, on the other hand, work hard to make their problems realistic, relevant and unambiguous. In this pursuit of singleness of meaning and relevancy, they are stymied by the genre's history and form, which carry with them the intention to create paradox and at best a shifting relationship to everyday reality.

What if we treated word problems in mathematics classes as if they were parables or riddles? Would this alter our intentions as mathematics educators or our students' perceptions of those intentions?

For example, if word problems were not considered disposable exercises (as they often are now) but as parables worthy of longer and deeper contemplation, we might spend a week considering a single word problem in all its considerations and implications. Students might be asked to comb older textbooks or even historical sources for word problems pointing to the same mathematical structures as the "parabolic" story under consideration.

They might consider changing certain features of the word problem while holding others unchanged and seeing whether this altered the mathematical relationships pointed to in the problem. They might try to project real-life situations in which recalling the word problem "parable" might be instructive or helpful or comforting.

And what if word problems were considered as riddles? First of all, a playful and perhaps competitive spirit would be invoked. Word play and double meanings would be welcomed rather than banned. A pleasurable oral-culture approach to a recreational use of word problems would take the place of our present, very serious approach to evaluation of student written knowledge.

Perhaps the simple suggestion that mathematical word problems be considered *as parables* or *as riddles*—the shift to the "as if" point of view that characterizes play and drama—may begin to engender a shift in thinking and in educational practice.

I want to offer some specific ideas to teachers working with word problems who would like to approach this genre in new ways. I am inspired by the work of British applied linguists Paul Davis and Mario Rinvolucri (1988). Davis and Rinvolucri considered second-language commonplace forms, generic forms, like dictations and language labs and worked to reframe them in new ways that would revitalize the genres by reworking them in a playful way. (Interestingly, Davis and Rinvolucri dedicate their book to Caleb Gattegno, "absent from the bibliographies but vividly present in the minds of many practitioners" (Davis & Rinvolucri, 1988, p. ii). Gattegno's work has been an inspiration for innovative pedagogy in both mathematics and language education in Britain and North America over the past fifty years.)

In their introduction to their book, *Dictation* (1988), writing about "a new methodology for an age-old exercise," Davis and Rinvolucri write:

> To brainstorm a new methodology for dictation we asked ourselves a number of basic questions.... *Who dictates?... Who chooses the texts?... How long should they be?...How should the voice dictating sound?... Must the listener write down everything?... Who corrects the dictation?*

(pp. 2–4)

The consideration of unconventional answers to questions like these generated scores of lively and unorthodox classroom exercises that form this book for language teachers. For example, Davis and Rinvolucri suggest that not only the teacher can "dictate" the text —students could dictate to one another or to the teacher or could listen to their own or other voices on a tape. Students could offer several choices of text, and the teacher choose. The text for dictation could be a single word, a whole passage, or a passage read in a continuous loop on a tape. The voice dictating could sound like a whisper or a shout; it might be singing the text or speaking it to a background of music. The listener might write down only selected bits of the text, perhaps only the parts they agree with, or listeners might write down the whole text plus their own reactions or change the text to what they would like it to say—and so on. By identifying the key features of a generic form (in terms of the language class dictation, the idea that *someone* reads *some kind of text* to *listeners* who *write it down* and *correct it*) and then playing with possible changes and inversions of these features, Davis and Rinvolucri have been able to infuse an old form with new energy. This re-visioning of old forms also appeals to students' and teachers' sense of humor and play, as we begin to work with the "world turned upside down" of familiar and sometimes stultifying forms set to new purposes and intentions without subverting their educational usefulness. Dictations in language classes *are* worth using.

> The students are active during … [and] after the exercise…. Dictation leads to oral communicative activities…. Dictation fosters unconscious thinking,… copes with mixed-ability groups [and] large groups…. Dictation will often calm groups,… is safe for the non-native teacher [and] is a technically useful exercise…. Dictation gives access to interesting text. (Davis & Rinvolucri, 1988, pp. 4–8)

Re-visioned dictations aim to retain and emphasize these

positive features while at the same time breaking with typical, perhaps petrified practices.

Similarly, the generic forms of mathematics education, including mathematical word problems, *are* worth using for the following reasons among others:

• **Word problems connect us with the history and cultural geography of mathematics,** going back continuously 4000 years to medieval and Renaissance Europe, the Islamic world, India and China and ancient Rome, Egypt and Babylon. Ancient and medieval word problems originating in many cultures can still be done by students today. Word problems offer us insights into the nature of mathematical cultures and intellectual developments through the use of primary-source material that is accessible, brief and familiar in form.

• **Word problems provide concrete visualizations of the abstract relationships of mathematics.** These visualizations may serve as archetypes for particular abstract concepts and, through their sensory imagery, serve as a "touchstone" and mnemonic aid for students in grasping mathematical ideas.

• **Word problems may offer clues to the development of abstract concepts** by hinting at their origins in "real-life" problems. Although, as shown earlier, the solutions to mathematical word problems do *not* map directly onto the solution of practical problems in everyday life, they do often point to the "situations" that, historically, led to the perception of abstract patterns and the development of new mathematical ideas. Working back and forth among representations of real-life situations, the perception of patterns in those situations, traditional word problems and abstract mathematics students can begin to understand what it is to be a mathematician. Rather than offer up mathematics only in a pre-made, "pre-cooked" form, we can create space for students to think mathematically and to create and appreciate the archetypal stories that embody mathematical ideas.

• **Word problems can be pleasurable if their imagery is appealing,** perhaps even nonsensical and if they are approached in a spirit of play. There is a strong connection between word problems and mathematical recreations, riddles and puzzles that may be invoked even in the classroom.
• **Word problems can "stay in the mind" and provide guidance in times of difficulty** when treated as the closely related genre of parable. If a particular word problem is seen as the exemplar of a whole class of problems and given time and attention accordingly, it can be made available to memory as an entrance point to that class of problems and the same word problem can be approached at different levels with students' growing mathematical sophistication.
• **Word problems can connect the world of mathematics with the world of story** and make contact with the very human need for narrative in what is often seen as a "cold" world of abstract formulations.
• **Word problems can help students and teachers understand generic forms in education** and provide a forum for the discussion of the revitalization of educational forms throughout schooling. A re-visioning of mathematical word problems can be a model of ways to work with old forms in new ways (rather than simply discarding the genres that embody our history as a culture).

What follows are three suggestions of ways that teachers could work with mathematical word problems in a different way:

(1) draw attention to the intentional ambiguities created when word problems set up a "resonant space" between story and mathematics;
(2) focus on the use of word problems as a way to establish prototypical mnemonic imagery for a mathematical concept; and
(3) focus attention on the genre and explore its boundaries.

Drawing Attention to Intentional Ambiguities in Word Problems

Mathematics is often "sold" to school students as a realm of certainty and absolute clarity, the one school subject in which there are no doubts, no ambiguities, no two ways about it. In math class, there is only one right answer. Many students and some teachers as well, value the mathematical world as a place to escape from the messiness and ambiguities inherent, for example, in human disciplines like literature and history. They seek a less complex space, where linear logic and a strict one-to-one match between word and meaning apply.

But mathematics is not unambiguous. In fact, ambiguities are often intentionally built in to mathematical symbolism to add the potential for layered richness to mathematical understanding (what would be called *subtext* in literary studies). These ambiguities frequently appear in places where an elementary mathematical concept has been recontextualized in light of a later, perhaps deeper new idea, where the earlier idea is reframed as a "special case" of the later one. (For example, the rational numbers are reframed as a special case of the real numbers, or Euclidean geometry is reframed as a special case of all possible geometries.)

In mathematical word problems, the gap between the story of the problem and any possible mathematical representation of that story immediately sets up a resonant space—a space of echo and "vibration" between the story and the mathematical model of that story, a space of ambiguity and slippage rather than a tight one-to-one matching or a certain fit. It is this gap, I think, that causes a great deal of anxiety for students who seek refuge from the messiness of the real in their math classroom.

Besides, the mathematical symbolism used in solving word problems is often ambiguous in itself, deliberately so and this "doubleness" adds richness to the interpretation of the story and its modeling. A teacher who can help students notice and value this ambiguity may allay some of the anxiety students feel and help them to appreciate some of the complex understandings that are available in mathematics.

An example of this kind of ambiguity comes from word problems involving the graphing of quadratic functions in senior secondary school math. The first type of word problem, known as "the diving board problem," is usually taught as a way to model an object's trajectory as a parabola on a Cartesian plane.

> On a forward somersault dive, Greg's height h metres above the water is given approximately by
> $h = -5t2 + 6t = 3$, where t is the time in seconds after he leaves the board.
> a) Find Greg's maximum height above the water.
> b) How long does it take him to reach the maximum height?
> c) How long is it before he enters the water?
> d) How high is the board above the water? (Kelly et al., 1989, p. 220)

The usual way that this problem is solved in school is to create an x-axis representing time in seconds and a y-axis representing height in metres. Students are taught to place the height of the diving board on the y-axis, use methods already learned to find the vertex (high point) and positive root of the quadratic (the point where the parabola crosses the x-axis on the positive side) and to interpret these, respectively, as the high point of the dive and the time the diver touches the surface of the water.

The strangeness of this solution is that all the elements of the graph thus created are ambiguous in their interpretations. The x-axis represents, all at once, the time taken from the start of the dive (where x equals zero seconds) to the moment the diver enters the water and the surface of the water itself. The y-axis represents the concept of the height above the surface of the water *and* a picture or diagram of the diving tower. The parabolic arc on the graph represents both the temporal trajectory of the diver (i.e., the diver's height above the water at any given time) *and* the diver's spatial trajectory, since the diver's path through space is also a parabola of similar dimensions. A reinterpreted x-axis and a slightly altered equation could represent the horizontal distance from the diving board rather than the time elapsed when the diver enters the water.

These ambiguities are intentional and emphasize the beauty of a mathematics where a horizontal line can, at once, stand as a picture of the surface of water and a representation of time's passing and that these two metaphors can be held simultaneously in the mind *and* produce correct answers about the diver's height at any time.

However, in another similar word problem, also included in the senior math program, the metaphoric link between the x-axis and the surface of water is severed:

> Example 1.
> A bridge over a river is supported by a parabolic arch which is 40m wide at water level. The maximum height of the arch is 16m.
> a) Write an equation to represent the arch.
> b) How high is the arch at a point 10m from the centre? (Kelly et al., 1990, p. 109)

In this case, the suggested graph of the bridge support has its vertex (high point) at the x-axis. If the x-axis were to represent the surface of the water as it did in the "diving problem," the bridge support would be entirely underwater (making this a very unusual bridge!). In this case, the x- and y-axes both represent spatial dimensions (height and width) and a horizontal line at $y=-16$ represents the surface of the water.

There is ambiguity at several levels involved in the consideration of these two word problems about parabolas. First, as mentioned above, lines on the graph may at once represent physical entities (the surface of the water) and more abstract quantities like distance and time. Second, the meaning these representations may shift or slip from one problem to the next. The x-axis is not *always* meant to represent the surface of water—in fact, it may sometimes be more convenient to make a line above or below it represent the surface of a river or a swimming pool. In the same way that students may have difficulty accepting the "variability" of meaning for variables in algebra (which may simultaneously or alternately

be used to represent a single unknown quantity, a range of unknown quantities, a placeholder for known constant(s), or an abstraction of the relationship between entities), they may have difficulty in accepting the ambiguity of graphic representations of
functions, which may shift in order to give "nice" answers to algebraic questions.

A further level of complexity in using Cartesian co-ordinate
geometry is the relationship between the x- and y-axes and our
sense of our own physicality, a relationship rarely addressed in
mathematics classrooms. Teachers observing their own and their
students' use of gesture when describing the graphs of functions
will notice that negative x-values are gestured to the left of the
body, positive values to the right; negative y-values are gestured
below the waist, positive values above it; the horizontal line $y=4$
is usually described by a gesture at chest height. Drawing attention to bodily metaphors embedded in Cartesian graphs is an interesting exercise for students and teachers. The y-axis is generally
taken as a metaphor for the vertical axis of the body or the spine;
the x-axis as an extension of the middle horizontal line of the
body or the waist; and the origin as the navel—a fitting origin indeed, at the umbilicus, related mythologically to the omphalos, the
navel and centre of the world in Greek mythology. (In a similar
way, the x-axis is also used metaphorically to represent the surface of the earth when we talk about the "roots" of functions.)

An exploration of the function of metaphor in the translation
of word problem stories to graphs and in the interpretation of the
graphs themselves is a way to acknowledge and explicitly value
the ambiguities built into mathematics (deliberately and as artefacts of its human history) and to give students a sense of the
richness of interpretation made possible by these multiple
meanings.

Using Word Problems to Develop Prototypical Imagery
for a Class of Problems

In chapter 6, students talked about the usefulness of word

problems in providing interesting or memorable imagery to attach to abstract mathematical concepts, which were seen as "dry" or unmemorable in themselves. Teachers can (and historically have) explicitly used word-problem imagery as a mnemonic device and a shorthand for referring to particular abstract concepts in a readily accessible way. By setting up a particular type of word problem as the prototype for a whole class of mathematical problems, a teacher can help students see the common mathematical structure being "pointed at" by the widely differing stories of a class of word problems and offer a mental image that offers a specific and generalizable example of that structure.

For example, the Dirlichet principle in discrete mathematics is also called the "pigeonhole principle," and the imagery of pigeons and pigeonholes makes the principle more readily accessible than its statement in the abstract. The Dirlichet principle can be stated in the following way:

> If n objects are put into p boxes ($1 \leq p \leq n$), then some box contains at least two of the objects.

Using the imagery of the pigeonhole, the Dirlichet principle can be more memorably stated in this way:

> If there are ten pigeons roosting in nine pigeonholes, there must be at least one pigeonhole with at least two pigeons in it.

A related, commonly used image for counting principles in discrete mathematics talks about "counting the fence posts or the spaces between the fence posts." The number of fence posts will always be one greater than the number of spaces between the posts and the question of which of these you are counting is significant in creating mathematical models of problems. The imagery of fence posts and pigeons is memorable and taken to be prototypical—as are images of shared pizzas or pies in the teaching of fractions, images of flagpoles and their shadows in teaching triangulation and so on.

In pre-algebraic understandings of mathematics, as discussed in chapter 7, the prototypical word problem was the *only* way of characterizing a class of problems. Even now, certain famous classes of problems are known by the name of their word-problem prototype—the "two trains" problem or the "cistern" problem, for example. It is significant that the "cistern" problem, in which a water tank is drained by two different-sized pipes, has a mathematical structure identical to the "two men paint a room" problem, in which two painters work at different speeds to complete a task. In fact, both of these problem types are usually referred to as variants of the "cistern" problem.

Tropfke (1980) has used this way of characterizing word problems by prototype to organize his epic work which traces the historical and geographic roots of many classes of mathematical word problems. They are classified by prototype in terms of "the 100 birds problem," "the messenger problem" and so on, although some of their instantiations may not actually be about birds or messengers.

A teacher can help students sort out and classify similar concepts by explicitly working on "attaching" contrasting prototypical word problem imagery to each concept. For example, in teaching a secondary school unit introducing probability, I found that by the end of the unit students had forgotten about the very basic "Fundamental Counting Principle" and were confusing it with other concepts in probability and combinatorics. The Fundamental Counting Principle states that

> if a task is made up of stages, the total number of possibilities for the task is given by $m \times n \times p \times \ldots$, where m is the number of choices for the first stage, n is the number of choices for the second stage, p is the number of choices for the third stage and so on.

The prototypical example often given for this principle is a story of a sandwich bar where customers have a choice of four kinds of bread, three kinds of topping and six kinds of filling—in this case, $(4 \times 3 \times 6) = 72$ different kinds of sandwich combinations could be made.

When I found that my students did not find the sandwich bar image memorable, I asked them each to think about an image related to this mathematical structure that they would remember. One student liked to think about four kinds of mascara, seven kinds of eye shadow, six kinds of lip liner and so on; another preferred to think about twelve video game superheroes, each with a choice of eight kinds of weapons, ten kinds of armor, etc. From then on, they referred to the Fundamental Counting Principle, respectively, as "the one about the makeup" or "the one about the weapons" and found it easier to remember. When we studied conditional probability, a word problem about the percentage of false negatives and false positives in a simple diabetes test struck us as prototypical of this concept. From then on, conditional probability questions were referred to by the group as "diabetes questions," and the structure of the original word problem was a memorable and accessible metaphor for other questions of this type.

Focusing on Word Problems as a Genre

In a workshop with elementary and secondary school teachers in the early stages of research for this book, I designed the following activity to test my initial hypotheses about the word-problem genre by pushing genre boundaries. This genre-awareness activity could be adapted for use in a middle school or high school classroom to spark discussion about word problems—what they are and are not, where they come from and what we expect of them.

In planning this genre-bending activity, I first identified some of the features that seemed to be central to the word problems genre—and then altered them, much in the same way that Davis and Rinvolucri explored the margins of the "dictation" genre by altering its features.

For example:

(a) Word problems have a three-constituent ordered structure

(set up, data and question). What if the order of those con-
stituents were altered, or if one or more of them were missing?
(b) Word problems are usually presented in written form.
What if they were presented orally or on audio- or videotape?
(c) Word problems are usually short—typically two or three
sentences. What if they were extraordinarily long?
(d) Word problems are usually written in prose form, following prose conventions of spelling, punctuation, etc. What if
they were written in verse or poetry, with unconventional
spellings, punctuation, etc.?
(e) Word problems are usually devoid of emotional content.
What if word problems were presented that contained emotive
prose?
(f) Word problems generally require an answer in words and
equations. What if the answer were to be in a different format—a drawing, a poem, a piece of music, etc.?

I assembled a number of texts that were both like and unlike
word problems in these ways—texts that were on the fringes of
the word problem genre—to present to the teachers I would be
working with. The texts chosen included the following:

(a) Texts that broke the convention of the three-component ordered structure of word problems included traditional English
riddles, which did not typically include a question component,
like the following:

> The fiddler and his wife,
> The piper and his mother,
> Ate three half-cakes, three whole cakes,
> And three quarters of another. (Opie & Opie, 1963, p. 72)

or the following, written by Lewis Carroll, which appears to
lack a data component:

> Dreaming of apples on a wall,

And dreaming often, dear,
I dreamed that, if I counted all,
—How many would appear? (Carroll, 1988, p. 733)

or another by Lewis Carroll, which lacks a question and also breaks convention (c) since it is excessively long and descriptive:

> When the king found that his money was nearly all gone and that he really *must* live more economically, he decided on sending away most of his Wise Men. There were some hundreds of them—very fine old men and magnificently dressed in green velvet gowns with gold buttons; if they *had* a fault, it was that they always contradicted one another when he asked for their advice—and they certainly ate and drank enormously. so, on the whole, he was rather glad to get rid of them. But there was an old law, which he did not dare to disobey, which said that there must always be
>
> "Seven blind of both eyes:
> Two blind of one eye:
> Four that see with both eyes:
> Nine that see with one eye." (Carroll, 1988, p. 734)

(b) Texts presented on audiotape rather than in print. I chose two passages from old movies which I recorded on audiocassette:

•A passage from the film *The Wizard of Oz* where the Scarecrow is awarded a diploma for brains by the Wizard. The scarecrow responds by reciting a mangled version of the Pythagorean Theorem, which I recorded.

• A passage from the Marx Brothers film, *Duck Soup*, in which Chico's character, a band leader, attempts to prove mathematically that it will cost Groucho's character less money for his band *not* to play than to play. (For example, Groucho would have to pay more to get the band *not* to rehearse than to rehearse.)

(a), (c) and (e) I wrote a number of unconventional word problems which used emotive language and upset the fixed order of
the three components (set-up, data, question) and made the
question a bit too long. For example:

> I deserve at least three pieces of pizza. I'm sure of it! I'm right, aren't
> I? Because Chris only wanted two pieces. I think they're trying to
> take what's mine and what kind of friends are they if they'd do that?
> There are nine of them, plus me and Chris. And they each took three
> and left me with only one! That's so wrong! And there were three
> large pizzas, each cut into ten. Even two pieces would be OK,
> but—one? That's insulting! And they are really selfish and immature.

(f) I used several of the riddles or brain-teasers from Remi
Charlip's children's book, *Arm in Arm* and asked participants
to *draw* the relationship shown and represent it algebraically.
For example:

> Isn't it better to be out in the cold snow saying, "Isn't it better to be
> out in the cold snow rather than in a warm bed?" rather than in a
> warm bed saying, "Isn't it better to be out in the cold snow rather
> than in a warm bed?"

> Isn't it better to be in a warm bed saying, "Isn't it better to be in a
> warm bed rather than out in the cold snow?" rather than out in the
> cold snow saying, "Isn't it better to be in a warm bed rather than out
> in the cold snow?" (Charlip, 1969/1997, pp. 4–5)

Participants in this workshop circulated among "stations"
where they were asked to work on these problems and to reflect
on whether these were word problems or not. Some interesting
observations:

• Many participants were put off by questions that included
emotive language and found themselves becoming embroiled in
emotional issues (for example, whether the question was
worded too aggressively) rather than working on the problem.

• Traditional riddles, which did not contain a question, left participants confused about what to do. In the riddle about "The fiddler and his wife, the piper and his mother," nearly everyone began adding the numbers given (three, three halves and three quarters). Once this was done, there was no further action anyone could think of taking, since the sum was not a whole number divisible by four. None suspected wordplay as a solution here. (The traditional solution to this riddle is that there are only three people involved, since the fiddler and his wife are the piper's parents.)

• Participants found it difficult but stimulating to work on problems recorded on audiotape and problems where a drawing was required.

• Most said that the problems presented to them both were and weren't word problems. They relied on the conventional format of word problems which was "transparent," or even invisible to them as math teachers and found that problems that broke with unspoken conventions were both frustrating and stimulating because of their novelty. By the end of the workshop they were certainly able to enunciate the features they expected of traditional word problems and to begin to think outside those conventions to some degree.

Playing with genre and even pushing its elements beyond genre limits may lead to unexpected insights. Why not take a playful approach to the traditional genres of mathematics education and what is more, why not let our students in on what we know about these genres and give them a chance to play with them too? Rather than forcing a choice for teachers, either to embrace traditions unthinkingly or discard traditional forms in a fever of reform, we could "try on" new contexts for old forms and encourage an awareness of the forms themselves. By playing with unfamiliar intentions for familiar forms, we may find renewed meanings and resonances for the genres of mathematics education.

Appendix
A Glossary of Terms from Linguistics, Discourse Analysis and Genre Analysis

Deixis: from the Greek word for "pointing" (as in "index"), refers to the process of pointing with words. Deixis studies the contextual referents for demonstratives ("this", "that"), pronouns ("I," "you," "it," etc.), verb tenses, context-referential adverbs of time and place ("then," "here") and "a variety of other grammatical features tied directly to the circumstances of utterance" (Levinson, 1983, p. 54).

Context of utterance is here referred to in terms of pragmatic indices, co-ordinates or reference points. For example, the deixis of verb tense is analyzed with reference to the time an utterance was spoken or written ("coding time") and the time it was heard or read ("receiving time"), which may or may not be distinct. Demonstratives, adverbs of time and place and verb tenses are described on a continuum that ranges from closest ("maximally proximal") to furthest away ("maximally distal") from a central point of reference ("deictic centre")—for example, some dialects of American English have three adverbs referring to locations increasingly distal from a deictic centre ("here," "there" and "yonder").

Discourse analysis: This term has been adopted by a large number of disciplines, including various branches of linguistics, literary studies, ethnography, sociology, film studies and artificial intelligence. Generally, discourse analysis refers to the structural analysis of stretches of "text" (in its broadest meaning) at a level larger than the sentence or utterance. The texts in question may range from spoken discourse in classrooms or courtrooms, to written texts like stories, novels, poems, letters or graffiti, to dialogue in film or theatre, to oral genres like storytelling, speech making, gossip, jokes and puns (see Coulthard, 1992; van Dijk, 1985a; van Dijk, 1985b).

The analytic methods that fall under the general heading "discourse analysis" are as heterogeneous as the texts they are used to analyze. Deborah Schiffrin (1994) writes that discourse analysis is "widely recognized as one of the most vast, but also one of the least defined, areas in linguistics" (p. 5) and goes on to describe six approaches currently used in discourse analysis methodology: **pragmatics**, speech act theory, interactional sociolinguistics, ethnography of communication, conversational analysis and variation analysis.

Genre analysis: The term "speech genre" was coined by Mikhail Bakhtin to describe "relatively stable types of utterances" (Bakhtin, 1986, p. 60). The notion of genre analysis has since been taken up in other areas of cultural analysis, notably film studies and literary criticism.

Bakhtin stresses that genres can be analyzed only by considering the whole of an utterance, including consideration of its thematic content, linguistic style (including lexical, syntactic and other grammatical features), its compositional structure, its expressiveness and its addressivity. Since decontextualized words and sentences lose this quality of addressivity, a purely atomistic formal linguistic approach cannot capture the features of a genre.

Gricean maxims: The study of **implicature** has a basis in ideas expressed by H. P. Grice in a series of Harvard lectures in 1967 (Grice, 1975, 1978). Grice looked for a set of assumptions underlying the efficient co-operative use of language. The five principles he found, including a general "co-operative principle" and four "(Gricean) maxims of conversation" are listed below.

1) *The co-operative principle*: Make your contribution such as is required, at the stage at which it occurs, by the accepted purpose or direction of the talk exchange in which you are engaged.

2) *The maxim of quality*: Try to make your contribution one that is true, specifically:
i) do not say what you believe to be false
ii) do not say that for which you lack adequate evidence.

3) *The maxim of quantity:*
i) Make your contribution as informative as is required for the current purposes of the exchange.
ii) do not make your contribution more informative than is required.

4) *The maxim of relevance:* Make your contributions relevant.

5) *The maxim of manner:* Be perspicuous and specifically:
i) avoid obscurity, ii) avoid ambiguity, iii) be brief and iv) be orderly

Grice's point is not that all speakers must follow these guidelines exactly, since it is obvious that no one speaks this way all the time. Rather, he says that when an utterance appears to be non-cooperative on the surface, we try to interpret it as co-operative at a deeper level. Levinson gives the following example:

A: Where's Bill?
B: There's a yellow VW outside Sue's house.
(Levinson, 1983, p. 102)

B's contribution, if taken literally, does not answer A's question and it might seem as if B were being uncooperative and changing the topic. However, if we assume that B is, at some deeper level, being cooperative and respecting the maxim of relevance, we try to make a connection between Bill's location and the location of a yellow VW and conclude that, if Bill has a yellow VW, he may be at Sue's house.

Implicature: "provides some explicit account of how it is possible to mean more than what is actually said (i. e., more than what is literally expressed by the conventional sense of the linguistic expressions uttered)." (Levinson, 1983, p. 97) For instance, Levinson gives the following example:

> A: Can you tell me the time?
> B: Well, the milkman has come.

and paraphrases what native speakers would understand by this exchange as follows:

> A: Do you have the ability to tell me the time of the present moment, as standardly indicated on a watch and if so please do so tell me.
> B: No, I don't know the exact time of the present moment but I can provide some information from which you may be able to deduce the approximate time, namely the milkman has come.

Implicature studies the mechanisms by which speakers of a language can understand utterances' unstated relationship to context and to the speakers and listeners involved in the conversation (or to the writers and readers involved in a written exchange).

Pragmatics: In Anglo-American linguistics, pragmatics is often defined as "the study of language usage" (Levinson, 1983, p. 5). This is a rather vague definition and allows for an unintentional amount of overlap between pragmatics and other areas like sociolinguistics, psycholinguistics, etc. Levinson (1983) struggles with alternative, more specific definitions and comes up with the following possibilities:

> Pragmatics is the study of those relations between language and context that are *grammaticalized* or encoded in the structure of a language. (p. 9)

> Pragmatics is the study of the relations between language and context … basic to an account of language understanding. (p. 21)

> Pragmatics is the study of **deixis** (at least in part), **implicature**, presupposition, speech acts and aspects of discourse structure. (p. 27)

References

Aaboe, A. (1964). *Episodes from the early history of mathematics.* Washington, DC: Mathematical Association of America.

Ainley, J. (1996). *Constructing purpose in mathematics classrooms.* Unpublished doctoral dissertation, University of Warwick, England.

Alberta Education. (1999). *Standards for Applied Mathematics 10: First draft for response.* Edmonton, AB: Alberta Education, Curriculum Standards Branch.

Alexander, B., Folk, S., Worth, J. & Kelly, B. (1989). *Mathquest 7.* Don Mills, ON: Addison-Wesley.

Bakhtin, M. M. (1986). *Speech genres and other late essays.* (V. W. McGee, Trans.) Austin, TX: University of Texas Press.

Berkenkotter, C. & Huckin, T. N. (1995). *Genre knowledge in disciplinary communication: Cognition/ culture/ power.* Hillsdale, NJ: Erlbaum.

Borasi, R. (1986). On the nature of problems. *Educational Studies in Mathematics, 17,* 125–141.

Brown, S., & Walter, M. (1990). *The art of problem posing.* Hillsdale, NJ: Erlbaum.

Burton, M. B. (1991). Grammatical translation-inhibitors in two classic word problem sentences. *For the Learning of Mathematics , 11* (1), 43–46.

Buscombe, E. (1970/1995). The idea of genre in the American cinema. In B. K. Grant (Ed.) (1995). *Film genre reader II.* Austin, TX: University of Texas Press, 11–25.

Campbell, K. K., & Jamieson, K. H. (1978). Form and genre in rhetorical criticism: An introduction. In K. K. Campbell & K. H. Jamieson (Eds.) (1978). *Form and genre: Shaping rhetorical action.* Falls Church, VA: The Speech Communication Association, 9–32.

Cardano, G. (1968: 1545). *The great art, or the rules of algebra.* (T. R. Witmer, Trans. & Ed.). Cambridge, MA: MIT University

Press.

Carroll, L. (1988: 1856). *The complete works of Lewis Carroll.* London: Penguin.

Charlip, R. (1969/1997). *Arm in arm: A collection of connections, endless tales, reiterations and other echolalia.* Berkeley, CA: Tricycle.

Coulthard, M. (Ed.) (1992). *Advances in spoken discourse analysis.* London: Routledge.

Davis, P., & Rinvolucri, M. (1988). *Dictation: New methods, new possibilities.* Cambridge: Cambridge University Press.

DES. (1982). *Mathematics counts (The Cockcroft report).* London: HMSO.

Devore, J. L. (1991). *Probability and statistics for engineering and the sciences.* Pacific Grove, CA: Brooks/Cole.

Ebos, F., Klassen, J., & Zolis, P. (1990). *Math matters: Book 3 (British Columbia edition).* Scarborough, ON: Nelson Canada.

Ellerton, N. F. (1989). The interface between mathematics and language. *Australian Journal of Reading, 12* (2), 92–102.

Fauvel, J., & Gray, J. (Eds.) (1987). *The history of mathematics: A reader.* London: Macmillan.

Gillings, R. (1972). *Mathematics in the time of the pharaohs.* Cambridge, MA: MIT University Press.

Grice, H. P. (1975). Logic and conversation. In P. Cole & J. L. Morgan (Eds.), *Syntax and semantics 3: Speech acts.* New York: Academic, 41–58.

Grice, H. P. (1978) Further notes on logic and conversation. In P. Cole (Ed.), *Syntax and semantics 9: Pragmatics.* New York: Academic, 113–28.

Harel, G., & Hoz, R. (1990). The structure of speed problems and its relation to problem complexity and isomorphism. *Journal of Structural Learning , 10* (3), 177–96.

Hermelink, H. (1978). Arabic recreational mathematics as a mirror of age-old cultural relations between Eastern and Western civilizations. In A. Y. Hassan, G. Karmi, & N. Namnum (Eds.), *Proceedings of the first international symposium for the history of Arabic science, April 5–12, 1976*. Vol. 2, Papers in European languages. Aleppo, Syria: Institute for the History of Arabic Science, Aleppo University.

Howson, A. G. (1995). *Mathematics textbooks: A comparative study of Grade 8 texts*. Vancouver, BC: Pacific Educational.

Høyrup, J. (1994). *In measure, number, and weight: Studies in mathematics and culture*. Albany, NY: State University of New York Press.

Hoz, R., & Harel, G. (1990). Higher order knowledge involved in the solution of algebra speed word problems. *Journal of Structural Learning* , 10 (4), 305–328.

Jamieson, K. M. (1975). Antecedent genre as historical constraint. *Quarterly Journal of Speech*, 61 (4), 406–15.

Johnson, M. (1992). *How to solve word problems in algebra*. New York: McGraw-Hill.

Joseph, G. G. (1992). *The crest of the peacock: Non-European roots of mathematics*. London: Penguin.

Kafka, F. (1961). *Parables and paradoxes*. New York: Schocken.

Keitel, C. (1989). Mathematics education and technology. *For the Learning of Mathematics*, 9 (1), 7–13.

Kelly, B., Carlow, C., Neufeld, R. V., Symington, J., & Worth, J. (1986) *Mathquest 5*. Don Mills, ON: Addison-Wesley.

Kelly, B., Alexander, B., & Atkinson, P. (1987a). *Mathematics 9*. Don Mills, ON: Addison-Wesley.

Kelly, B., Alexander, B., & Atkinson, P. (1987b). *Mathematics 10*. Don Mills, ON: Addison-Wesley.

Kelly, B., Alexander, B., Atkinson, P. & Swift, J. (1989). *Mathematics 11: British Columbia edition*. Don Mills, ON: Addison-Wesley.

Kelly, B., Alexander, B., Atkinson, P. & Adams, R.A. (1990). *Mathematics 12: British Columbia Edition*. Don Mills, ON: Addison-Wesley.

Klein, J. (1968). *Greek mathematical thought and the origin of algebra*. New York: Dover.

Kubala, T. S. (1973). *Practical problems in mathematics for electri-*

cians. Albany, NY: Delmar.

Lamarque, P., & Olsen, S. H. (1994). *Truth, fiction and literature: A philosophical perspective.* Oxford: Clarendon.

Lave, J. (1988). *Cognition in practice: Mind, mathematics and culture in everyday life.* Cambridge: Cambridge University Press.

Lave, J. (1992). Word problems: A microcosm of theories of learning. In P. Light & G. Butterworth (Eds.), *Context and cognition: Ways of learning and knowing.* New York: Harvester Wheatsheaf, 74–92.

Levinson, S. (1983). *Pragmatics.* Cambridge: Cambridge University Press.

Lincoln, Y. S. & Guba, E. G. (1985). *Naturalistic inquiry.* Newbury Park, CA: SAGE Publications.

Mangan, C. (1989). Choice of operation in multiplication and division word problems: A developmental study. *Journal of Structural Learning, 10,* 73–77.

Marks, D. (1994). A guide to more sensible word problems. *Mathematics Teacher, 87* (8), 610–11.

Maxwell, J. (1988). Hidden messages. In D. Pimm (Ed.), *Mathematics, teachers and children.* London: Hodder & Stoughton, 118–21.

May, J. R. (1976). *The pruning word: The parables of Flannery O'Connor.* Notre Dame, IN : University of Notre Dame Press.

Menon, R. (1993, April). *The role of context in student-constructed questions.* Paper presented at AERA annual meeting, Atlanta, GA.

Miller, C. R. (1984). Genre as social action. *Quarterly Journal of Speech, 70,* 151–67.

Miller, J. H. (1990). *Tropes, parables, performatives: Essays on twentieth-century literature.* London: Harvester Wheatsheaf.

Muller, E. (1994, December). Morocco for ICOTS 4. In *Newsletter of the Canadian Mathematics Education Study Group.* (Available from David Reid, Acadia University, Wolfville, Nova Scotia).

NCTM. (1970). *A history of mathematics education in the United States and Canada.* Washington, DC: National Council of Teachers of Mathematics.

NCTM. (1989). *Professional standards for teaching mathematics.* Reston, VA: National Council of Teachers of Mathematics.

Neale, S. (2000). *Genre and Hollywood.* London: Routledge.

Nesher, P. & Katriel, T. (1977). A semantic analysis of addition and subtraction word problems in arithmetic. *Educational Studies in Mathematics, 8,* 251–269.

Nunes, T., Schliemann, A. D. & Carraher, D. W. (1993). *Street mathematics and school mathematics.* Cambridge: Cambridge University Press.

Oden, T. (1978). Preface. In S. A. Kierkegaard, *Parables of Kierkegaard.* Princeton, NJ : Princeton University Press.

Olivastro, D. (1993). *Ancient puzzles.* New York: Bantam.

Ontario Ministry of Education & Training. (1999). *The Ontario curriculum: Grades 9 and 10 mathematics.* Toronto, ON: Ontario Ministry of Education & Training, Queen's Park.

Opie, I. & Opie, P. (1963). *The Puffin book of nursery rhymes.* London: Penguin.

Ormell, C. (1991). How ordinary meaning underpins the meaning of mathematics. *For the Learning of Mathematics, 11* (1), 25–30.

Palmer, J. (1991). *Potboilers: Methods, concepts and case studies in popular fiction.* London: Routledge.

Pimm, D. (1987). *Speaking mathematically: Communication in mathematics classrooms.* London: Routledge & Kegan Paul.

Pimm, D. (1995). *Symbols and meanings in school mathematics.* London: Routledge.

Pinder, R. (1987). *Why don't teachers teach like they used to?* London: Hilary Shipman.

Plane, H. (1990). Translating into algebra. In J. Fauvel (Ed.), *History in the mathematics classroom.* (C. Guillerme & C. Weeks, Trans.). Leicester, England: The Mathematical Association, 59–72.

Prestage, S. & Perks, P. (1992). Mathematics. In P. Ribbins (Ed.), *Delivering the National Curriculum: Subjects for secondary schooling.* Harlow, Essex: Longman, 53–76.

Puchalska, E., & Semadeni, Z. (1987). Children's reactions to verbal arithmetical problems with missing, surplus or contradictory data. *For the Learning of Mathematics, 7* (3), 9–16.

Radatz, H. (1984). Schwierigkeiten der Anwendung arithmetischen Wissens am Beispiel des Sachrechnens. In J. H. Lorenz, Aulis Verlag Deubner, Köln (Eds.) *Lernschwierigkeiten: Forschung und Praxis.* (Untersuchungen zum Mathematikunterricht, IDM Universität Bielefeld, Band 10), 17-29.

Rosch, E. (1975). Cognitive representations of semantic categories. *Journal of Experimental Psychology (General), 104,* 192–233.

Roth, M. (1996). Where is the context in contextual word problems?: Mathematical practices and products in grade 8 students' answers to story problems. *Cognition and Instruction, 14* (4), 487–527.

Rowland, T. (1992). Pointing with pronouns. *For the Learning of Mathematics, 12* (2), 44–48.

Rowland, T. (1999). Pronouns in mathematics talk: Power, vagueness and generalization. *For the Learning of Mathematics, 19* (2).

Schiffrin, D. (1994). *Approaches to discourse.* Oxford: Blackwell.

Schoenfeld, A. H. (1985). *Mathematical problem solving.* Orlando, FL: Academic.

Scott, C. T. (1965). *Persian and Arabic riddles: A language-centred approach to genre definition.* The Hague: Mouton & Co.

Shah, I. (1981). *The magic monastery: Analogical and action philosophy of the Middle East and Central Asia.* London: Octagon.

Singmaster, D. (1988). Some early source in recreational mathematics. In C. Hay (Ed.), *Mathematics from manuscript to print 1300–1600.* Oxford: Clarendon Press, 195–208.

Smith, B. (1988). Towards a problem-solving school. In D. Pimm (Ed.), *Mathematics, teachers and children.* London: Hodder & Stoughton, 22–42.

Sobchack, T. (1975/ 1995). Genre film: A classical experience. In B. K. Grant (Ed.) (1995). *Film genre reader II.* Austin, TX: University of Texas Press, 102–113.

Sowder, L. (1989). Searching for affect in the solution of story problems in mathematics. In D. B. McLeod & V. M. Adams (Eds.), *Affect and mathematical problem solving: A new perspective.* New York: Springer-Verlag, 104–113.

Stewart, J. (1991). *Calculus: Second edition.* Pacific Grove, CA: Brooks/Cole Publishing.

Swales, J. M. (1990). *Genre analysis.* Cambridge: Cambridge University Press.

Swetz, F. J. (1987). *Capitalism and arithmetic.* La Salle, IL: Open Court.

Swetz, F. J., & Kao, T. I. (1977). *Was Pythagoras Chinese?* Reston, VA: National Council of Teachers of Mathematics.

Tropfke, J. (1980). *Geschichte der Elementarmathematik, 4. Auflage: Band 1: Arithmetik und Algebra.* Berlin: De Gruyter.

Tudor, A. (1973/ 1995). Genre. In B. K. Grant (Ed.) (1995). *Film genre reader II.* Austin, TX: University of Texas Press, 3–10.

van der Waerden, B. L. (1954). *Science awakening.* (A. Dresden, Trans.). Groningen, Holland: P. Noordhoff .

van Dijk, T. A. (Ed.) (1985a). *Handbook of discourse analysis volume 3: Discourse and dialogue.* London: Harcourt Brace Jovanovitch.

van Dijk, T. A. (Ed.) (1985b). *Discourse and literature.* Amsterdam: John Benjamins.

Wickelgren, W. A. (1974). *How to solve problems: Elements of a theory of problems and problem solving.* San Francisco: W. H. Freeman.

Index

F

fiction, 34–35, 134
film studies, 15–20, 134
folklore studies, 21
folktales, 122, 138
force, locutionary, illocutionary
    and perlocutionary, 19, 31–34,
    44, 47, 49, 134
Frege & Strawson, 34
French immersion, 99
Fundamental Counting Principle,
    148–149

G

Gattegno, Caleb, 139
generative examples. *See* examples,
    illustrative and generative
genre, 4–12, 13–24, 26–27, 30, 33,
    34, 39–43, 47–51, 54, 87, 121,
    133–139, 142, 149–154,
    155–156; genre analysis, 114,
    156; genre, interdisciplinary
    construct of, 16; genre,
    rhetorical, 23, 49; genres,
    speech, 13–15
genre films, 16
geometry, 130
Greek mathematics, 116, 118–120,
    130
Grice, H. P., 87
Gricean maxim, 32, 37, 39, 120, 134,
    156–157

H

hermeneutics, 45
history of the word-problem genre,
    114–132, 136
Høyrup, Jens, 94, 118–123

I

illustrative examples. *See* examples,
    illustrative and generative
imagery, 73, 85, 98, 104, 109, 112,
    120, 130, 136, 141–142, 147,
    148
imitation, 19, 133
Indian mathematics, 11, 62, 114, 136
intentions, 7–9, 12, 19, 21, 31, 39,
    47–52, 53–55, 66, 68, 79, 80,
    84–88, 92, 95–98, 106,
    111–112, 134–140, 154
interdisciplinary construct of genre.
    See genre, interdisciplinary
    construct of
interviewing techniques, 47
Iran, 126
Islamic world, mathematics of, 62,
    114, 122, 130, 136, 141

J

Jamieson, K. H. , 22, 49

K

Kafka, Franz, 43, 44
Keitel, Christine, 82
Kierkegaard, Søren, 44
Klein, Jacob, 119

eXtreme teaching
rigorous texts for troubled times

Joe L. Kincheloe and Danny Weil
General Editors

Books in this series will provide practical ideas on classroom practice for teachers and teacher educators that are grounded in a profound understanding of the social, cultural, political, economic, historical, philosophical, and psychological contexts of education as well as in a keen sense of educational purpose. Within these contextual concerns contributors will address the ferment, uncertainty, and confusion that characterize the troubles of contemporary education. The series will focus specifically on the act of teaching. While the topics addressed may vary, EXtreme Teaching is ultimately a book series that addresses new, rigorous, and contextually informed modes of classroom practice. Authors will bring together a commitment to educational and social justice with a profound understanding of a rearticulation of what constitutes compelling scholarship. The series is based on the insight that the future of progressive educational reform rests at the intersection of socio-educational justice and scholarly rigor. Authors will present their conceptions of this rigorous new pedagogical frontier in an accessible manner that avoids the esoteric language of an "in group." In this context, the series editors will make use of their pedagogical expertise to introduce pedagogical ideas to student, teacher, and professional audiences. In this process, they will explain what they consider the basic concepts of a field of study, developing their own interpretive insights about the domain and how it should develop in the future. Very few progressive texts exist to introduce individuals to rigorous and complex conceptions of pedagogical practice: thus, authors will be expected to use their contextualized interpretive imaginations to introduce readers to a creative and progressive view of pedagogy in the field being analyzed.

For additional information about this series or for the submission of manuscripts, please contact:

Joe L. Kincheloe & Danny Weil
c/o Peter Lang Publishing, Inc.
275 Seventh Avenue, 28th floor
New York, New York 10001

To order other books in this series, please contact our Customer Service Department:
(800) 770-LANG (within the U.S.)
(212) 647-7706 (outside the U.S.)
(212) 647-7707 FAX

Or browse online by series at *www.peterlangusa.com*